Making the Most of Your Money

PERSONAL FINANCE GUIDES

In the same series:

Don't Pay Too Much Tax If You're An Employee
David Williams

Don't Pay Too Much Tax If You're Self–Employed
David Williams

Running Your Own Business
David Williams

Don't Pay Too Much Inheritance Tax
Tony Foreman and Wendy Gray

Making the Most of Your Money

Helen Pridham

NICHOLAS BREALEY
PUBLISHING

LONDON

First published in Great Britain by
Nicholas Brealey Publishing Limited in 1995
21 Bloomsbury Way
London WC1A 2TH

© Allied Dunbar Assurance plc, 1995

ISBN   1-85788-095-1

British Library Cataloguing-in-Publication Data
A catalogue record for this book is available from the British Library.

Produced by Frere Publishing Services, 2 Whitehorse Street, London W1
Printed and bound in Finland by Werner Soderstrom, Oy.

Contents

1 Making the most of what you've got

Money is something we would all like more of. Many people hope one day they may win the National Lottery or come up trumps with Premium Bonds. Yet often they do not make the most of what they have got already. Research has shown that investors are wasting millions of pounds in tax alone by not putting their savings in the most tax efficient investments.

Making the most of your money doesn't just mean paying less tax or getting the highest returns on your savings. It also means protecting what you have got against loss. And if you really want to improve your finances, going right back to basics to check, for example, that you have the best bank account to meet your needs and examining the effectiveness of all your existing financial arrangements can bring considerable savings.

Then there are your hopes and aspirations for the future. By using your current income and resources in a planned way now you stand a better chance of being able to achieve future goals. At the same time, it is important to retain flexibility so you can deal with changes in your circumstances. The need to be able to take account of change has become increasingly evident in recent years. Certain things which were once taken for granted - such as secure employment and a reasonable state retirement pension - are turning out to be anything but guaranteed.

Another reason to retain flexibility is that new opportunities are always presenting themselves as a result of increasing competition in the financial services field among banks, building societies and insurance companies.

What you cannot afford to do nowadays is to sit back uncritically and rely on others, be they bank managers, employers or the state, to look after your financial interests. If you want to be sure of getting the best deals for you and your family, you have to take control.

How much control do you have of your financial affairs at present? Have a look through some of the main changes that have occurred in recent years to see if you have taken appropriate action.

ARE YOU IN CONTROL?

Your job:
>   The combined effect of the recession and the privatisation of public services resulted in many companies slimming down their workforces. This has made redundancy and early retirement commonplace. Are you prepared if it happens to you?
>   More people are turning to self-employment. There has been an increase in part-time working and employment on short term contracts. The general feeling is that 'jobs for life' no longer exist. If you have become self-

employed, have you taken steps to ensure your future security?

Your home:

Until a few years ago buying a home was not only a way of getting a roof over your head but also a surefire investment. But at the end of the 1980s many people saw their dreams shattered - property prices fell. At the same time, mortgage rates took off like a rocket and questions were also raised about whether endowments would provide homeowners with enough to repay their mortgages at the end of the term. Many new mortgage products came onto the market including fixed rate mortgages. Have you reviewed your mortgage lately to see whether you could benefit from a mortgage switch? If you have an endowment, is it on target to repay your mortgage?

Interest rates:

Interest rates have yo-yoed wildly during the 1980s and 90s. Between 1989 and 1994, rates on building society instant access accounts fell from 14% to 4% gross. Did you make sure your savings were in the most competitive account?

Inflation:

Rising prices continue to eat away at the purchasing power of our money. Though inflation is low now compared with the 1970s and early 1980s, it is something which should not be ignored. As recently as 1990, inflation was standing at 10.9% - enough to reduce the value of your cash by two thirds over ten years. Are your savings protected against inflation?

Your pension:

A number of scandals have hit the pensions

industry in recent years. Perhaps the most shocking was the discovery that Robert Maxwell had plundered his company's pension funds leaving employees and ex-employees with little or no pension. But then came the news that personal pensions had been missold to members of good occupational pension schemes or low earners within the State Earnings Related Scheme (SERPS). But even if you are not affected by such scandals, you could find that your pension does not live up to your expectations. Have you reviewed your pension arrangements lately?

The Welfare State:

In its efforts to reduce the burgeoning cost of social security benefits, the Government is cutting back on benefits and encouraging individuals to make their own provision for retirement and to protect themselves against long term sickness.

State sickness benefits are being cut back from April 1995. Qualification for benefits is also to be made tougher. The elderly are already expected to pay for their own long term care. Have you protected your income against long term sickness? Have you thought of making provision to cover the cost of long term care?

Education:

It has always been necessary to pay your way if you wanted private education for your children. But now parents are being asked for greater contributions towards the cost of supporting children through higher education. Some universities may start charging extra fees. If you have children, have you started making provision?

**WHERE TO GO
FROM HERE**

The aim of this book is to help you deal with such situations as effectively as possible. The best way to do this is to develop good financial habits. The key to good money management is to have a detailed overview of your present financial position and to set yourself clear financial objectives. This is the reason that financial advisers nowadays are obliged to carry out financial 'fact-finds' before selling anything to you to ensure they know enough about you to give good advice. So before going any further, you should undertake your own financial self analysis. This is a three stage process.

THE FIRST STAGE:

The first stage is to carry out your own do-it-yourself fact-find. If you are well organised you may already have all the relevant information written down, though it is important to check that it is all up to date. If not, doing this financial stocktake can be an educational exercise. Many of us tend to accumulate a variety of financial baggage over the years - the odd savings policy and building society account, perhaps bits of pension from previous jobs - and then forget their true worth or at least put off doing anything about them. Seeing it all down in black and white may in itself spur you into action.

The other functions of this exercise are to help highlight where you can organise your finances more effectively and to show up any gaps that need to be filled. Some things may become immediately obvious, such as the need to check out old building society accounts to make sure you are still getting a good return or to top up your pension contributions.

The following is a checklist of what your financial fact-find should include :

1. Your Home:

If you own your own home, note its approximate present market value (ads in the local press for similar properties should help your estimate or ask a local estate agent for advice). Then write down the size of your mortgage and deduct this amount from the market value to get an estimate of your 'equity' in the property. Despite sluggish or falling house prices in recent years, many families still have homes worth more than their mortgages.

Give details of your mortgage lender and the current rate of interest you are paying. Also note what method of repayment you are using and when you expect to clear your loan. You will need this information in order to establish whether you can save money by switching to a different mortgage lender or by repaying your loan early.

Finally, write down details of your home buildings and contents insurance policies. Don't skimp on insurance. It is important to protect what you have got, otherwise if there were a fire, you'd be left with little.

2. Other Assets:

Make a note of any valuable possessions you have such as a car, jewellery, or a second home. Then list your savings and investments (other than pensions) starting with ready cash deposits such as bank and building society accounts, going on to National Savings products and insurance savings policies, and then any shares, unit trusts, investment bonds or Personal Equity Plans if you have them. Also note the rate of interest you are currently earning on your deposits, the maturity date of any fixed term investments and the original and current value of other holdings. If you are self-employed, you should also note down any business assets.

3. Your Future Pension:

If you are not already retired, you should be setting money aside towards your future pension. Write down any provision you have accumulated so far, whether through membership of your current or previous employers' schemes or your own personal pension plan. Make a note of how much you are currently contributing. It is most important to keep these contributions at a realistic level. Later in the book we will be looking at how you can do this.

4. Debts:

Put down any outstanding loans you may have other than your mortgage - your regular credit card debt, bank loans, car purchase loans or other credit agreements, plus any impending tax demand if you are self employed, and any business loans.

5. Protection:

How well protected is your family against possible financial hardship arising from death or ill health? List any life insurance, income protection insurance, critical illness cover, or medical expenses cover you may have.

Once you have completed your financial fact-find, you will be in a better position to plan effectively for the future. You can, for example, calculate your 'net worth' by adding the equity in your property to your other assets and deducting your debts. Another important part of the picture, though, is your 'cash flow' position - how your income matches up to your expenditure.

To find out how well you are coping financially at present you need to take a detailed look at your income and outgoings. So write down your income and that of your partner. As well as recording the income from your job or from a pension, don't forget to add any regular investment income you receive. Make a note too of any fringe benefits you get from an employer, such as a company car, or free medical expenses insurance which effectively boosts your income by cutting down your need to spend your own money.

The other side of the equation is your expenditure. Once again, writing it all down can be very educational. Many people get a surprise when they realise how much they spend on certain things. This exercise can also help you to quantify how much you can afford to save. If you have retired or been made redundant, use this method to work how much income you need from your investments.

On the next page there is a budget list to help you:

WHAT YOU SPEND

Work out an annual figure for each item

HOUSEHOLD
Mortgage/Rent	£......
Gas	£......
Electricity	£......
Water	£......
Community Charge	£......
Telephone	£......
Food & Drink	£......
Repairs & Maintenance	£......
Other	£......

TRANSPORT
Petrol	£.......
Road Tax	£.......
Car Service	£.......
Repairs	£.......
AA/RAC	£.......
Fares	£.......
Other	£.......

INSURANCE/SAVINGS
Motor	£......
Household	£......
Life assurance	£......
Medical	£......
Pension	£......
Savings	£......
Other	£......

ENTERTAINMENT
TV Licence	£.......
Cable/Satellite Sub.	£.......
Club Sub.	£.......
Hobbies	£.......
Theatre/cinema	£.......
Holidays	£.......
Other	£.......

CHILDREN
School fees	£......
Upkeep at College	£......
Clubs/Hobbies	£.....
Savings	£......
Other	£......

PERSONAL
Clothing	£.......
Hairdressers	£.......
Other	£.......

MISCELLANEOUS
Birthdays/Christmas	£.......
Other	£.......

TOTAL ANNUAL EXPENDITURE ....

The third stage in the process is to decide on your immediate financial priorities and future goals. This will show you what action you need to take next and what plans to make for the future. Naturally your needs and goals will change as your life progresses. No two people's lives are exactly the same but here are some typical examples of the financial problems people face at different ages to start you off on your own list.

THE THIRD STAGE:

The 20s:

Immediate:	Pay back student debts
	Decide on best way to borrow
Future:	Save up to buy a home
	Find a mortgage

The 30s and 40s:

Immediate:	Maximise income by minimising tax bills
	Make sure family is financially secure
	Fund children's school bills
	Move to larger property with larger mortgage
Future:	Provide for children's higher education
	Move to self-employment/start a business
	Build up a pension

The 50s:

Immediate:	Make a will if you have not already done so
	Build up investments
Future:	Boost pension
	Early retirement

The 60s:

Immediate:	Invest for income
	Check tax position

Future: Make sure capital keeps pace
               with inflation
               Inheritance tax planning
               Buy long term care insurance

The 70s and 80s:
Immediate: Review will
               Maximise income
Future: Pay for long term care
               Pass on wealth to children and
               grandchildren

Once you have considered your own objectives,
it is a good idea to prioritise them in order of
their importance to you. Any such steps you take
will all help to make the attainment of these
goals easier because you will be able to tailor
your financial arrangements accordingly.

WOMEN AND MONEY

Do women have different financial needs and
objectives to men? Judging by the number of
money books that have been written specially
for women on this subject (including one by this
author), the answer would appear to be yes.
However, these books invariably deal with the
same matters that are found in every other book
on the subject. Their main aim has been to
provide women with more information and give
them the confidence to deal with financial
decisions they may have previously left to men.

Nowadays women are less likely to need
confidence building. The majority work in paid
employment and have become used to financial
decision-making. Not only are they making
decisions about their own affairs, but they
expect to share in any decision-making with
their partner which affects them jointly. But they
still need the information on which to base
their decisions. The bulk of this book is of equal
relevance to men and women.

Where there are differences in the financial needs of women and men, they tend to arise from the difference in women's career patterns after they have had children. Since women still tend to take primary responsibility for childcare, their career is often interrupted for several years, either completely or by part-time work.

Many women underestimate the impact which this interruption has on their financial position, particularly on their pension prospects. For this reason, a chapter has been devoted to the problems women face in providing themselves with an adequate pension and ways of overcoming them. It also deals with the difficulties which women can encounter when a marriage or relationship breaks down, or a partner dies.

2 *Cash management*

M anaging your cash effectively now can help you to achieve future financial goals. So it is important not to overlook the basic financial building blocks such as making sure you have the right bank account and that you always borrow as cheaply as possible. You can save considerable amounts of money on these services if you make the right choices.

A bank account is the cornerstone of every adult's financial life nowadays. But banks can make astronomic charges. Fortunately mounting competition in recent years has provided more choice. Yet many people are still reluctant to switch bank accounts even though they could save pounds by doing so. If you have been with the same bank for some years, it is certainly worth checking out whether you could get a better deal elsewhere. If you are someone who goes overdrawn from time to time, getting the right account is vital. In this chapter we look at the main points to consider when choosing an account.

Overdrafts can be a very expensive way of borrowing money. We consider ways of avoiding them and look at cheaper alternatives. There are plenty of different ways of borrowing money but it is important to compare costs on a like for like basis and to make sure you do not overstretch yourself.

Besides the banks, a growing number of building societies now offer current accounts on competitive terms. Telephone banking and home banking via computer are also becoming increasingly popular. Each account has different terms, some pay interest and some don't. There is no single bank account that is right for everybody. Much will depend on how you conduct your account. The important thing is to find one which matches your needs.
What are your needs?

GETTING THE RIGHT BANK ACCOUNT

Do you always stay in credit?

You need an account which pays good interest. You won't have to pay bank charges but look out for additional charges, such as providing duplicate statements. And don't leave too much in your account, you can get better interest rates elsewhere.

Do you sometimes overdraw without asking your bank first?

You need an account which doesn't make excessive charges for bouncing cheques or sending warning letters. Some accounts even have a modest free overdraft limit. Before switching consider asking your bank for an agreed overdraft limit, find out the terms and conditions.

Do you have an agreed overdraft which you make use of often?

You need an account with no overdraft fees for agreed overdrafts and a competitive overdraft interest rate.

Do you find it difficult to get to your branch?

You need an account which gives you access to plenty of cash machines and offers telephone banking.

Are you running a small business?

Most banks now offer a packaged account for small businesses with turnovers of under £100,000 p.a. with set tariffs - usually a monthly or quarterly charge and a per item price. The best one for you will depend on the nature of your business, e.g. if you handle a lot of cash and need a night safe facility or mainly handle cheques. If you are just starting up, find a bank that will give you a period of free banking.

Whatever type of account you need it is vital to shop around. Publications which will assist you and make this process easier are *Which?* magazine - it normally carries out an annual review of current account charges and also very importantly examines the standard of service banks provide as well (your local library will have a copy) - and *Moneyfacts*, a monthly publication with lists of all current accounts and interest bearing cheque accounts. It has a quarterly sister publication *Business Moneyfacts* which gives details of small business accounts.

SWITCHING BANK ACCOUNTS

Many people avoid making the switch because they do not want the hassle but nowadays banks will often supply a transfer pack to help you through the process with instructions about what to do and pre-printed letters, etc. to make it all easier. If not, here's what to do:

1. Open your new account. Bear in mind it will probably take four to eight weeks to make a full transition, so don't close your old account until you are sure the process is complete.

2. Make a list of direct payments made to your account - salary, pension, child benefit, share dividends etc. and write to the organisations concerned giving details of your new account and when you want them to switch payments. Give them at least four weeks notice. Keep a copy of your letters.

3. Ask your old bank or building society for a list of direct debits and standing orders from your old account. It must send you this information but may make a charge.

4. You will need to take different action for standing orders and direct debits:

Standing orders:
Give a list of your standing orders to your new bank and ask it to start paying them from a date when you know your new account will have started receiving direct payments such as your salary. Cancel the standing orders at your old bank.

Direct debits:
Write to everyone you pay by direct debit asking for a new direct debit mandate form. Complete the forms and return them to those organisations making sure that they will be paid when there is sufficient in your new account to cover them. Write to your old bank confirming that you have cancelled your direct debits. (Don't worry too much about over-payments made during the changeover, you will get a refund if things go wrong.)

5. After all payments into and out of your old account have been switched to your new account, write to your old bank asking for your account to be closed and the remaining balance transferred to your new account.

HOW TO AVOID COSTLY OVERDRAFTS

Most banks charge you a lot more if you go overdrawn without asking than if you have an agreed overdraft limit - interest charged can be as much as three times as high, monthly standing overdraft fees are higher and you will also be charged around £20 for each cheque you write which bounces, as well as for direct debits or standing orders that are due while your account is overdrawn.

So how can these charges be kept to a minimum? If you are someone who slips into the red by mistake - try to keep a closer eye on your balance. Use a cash machine to check your running balance, or ring up if your account offers telebanking.

Remember to leave enough time between paying cheques in and drawing money against them. Find out how many days your bank takes to clear them. Try to delay your spending if you think you may not have enough in your account to cover it. Bear in mind the charging period on your account, because if your overdraft straddles two such periods even for a day or two you could be charged the monthly overdraft fee twice over.

If you find that it is heavy quarterly or annual bills, such as fuel bills or insurance premiums, which tend to push you into overdraft, consider switching to monthly payments, though always check out whether any extra charge for this facility is reasonable.

Using your credit card can be a good way of bridging a temporary gap in bank finances. You can get cash with your card as well as using it to pay for goods and services and even though you will incur an immediate charge for cash it will normally be cheaper than an unauthorised overdraft.

But if going into the red looks unavoidable, get your bank's agreement first. This will save you money and the embarrassment of cheques which bounce. You may be able to arrange this facility over the phone. Alternatively, consider whether another form of borrowing may be more appropriate.

Sensible use of credit has advantages. It can help you to budget and stretch your money further or meet unexpected costs. But you must be careful to keep your borrowing within reasonable limits and make sure that you get the best possible terms. This is easier said than done. Offers of instant credit abound in every high street and come unsolicited through the post. These offers may be convenient but not the cheapest.

BORROWING

Some borrowing may be unavoidable but before taking out credit always consider the alternatives.

Do you really need the item now, why not wait until you have saved enough?
Unless you can get interest free credit, remember that you will be paying, say, 20% - 30% more if you pay by credit rather than cash. You will also have the extra worry of meeting the repayments. If you wait until you can afford to pay in cash you will save yourself money and worry.
Why not use your savings?
It may be a good idea to use your rainy day savings from your bank or building society. You will pay a higher rate of interest for

credit than you can earn on this money. Then instead of making repayments on your loan, you can build up your savings again.

Could a relative help you out?

A relative may be happy to give you a loan if you ask nicely, perhaps even interest free. But agree the arrangements for repayment and stick to them if you want to avoid family strife.

THE COST

It is important to compare the interest charged for different forms of credit but other factors should also be considered.

The APR:

All lenders must show the cost of borrowing in the form of an APR (annual percentage rate). They must all work it out in the same way. It must include not only the interest but any other charges, such as arrangement fees as well. It also takes into account how and when payments are made. This enables you to make direct comparisons between one form of borrowing and another. Generally, the lower the APR the lower the cost. But always check that it is an APR that is being quoted, sometimes monthly or flat rates of interest are used as well and they sound a lot less.

The cost to you:

When you are comparing APRs, make sure the repayment periods are the same. As its name says the APR is the cost of credit over one year at a time. If you repay a loan over two years, the total cost will be more than if you repay over one year, even if the APR is lower.

Comparing **credit cards** with other

repayment methods on the basis of their APRs can also be misleading because no account is taken of the interest-free periods. And if you clear a debt within a few months, the cost will be less than the APR suggests.

When comparing credit deals remember to check whether the interest rate is **fixed** or **variable**. If it is variable and interest rates go up during the repayment term, this will increase the cost. A fixed rate has the advantage that you know exactly what your repayments will be, which is useful if you are on a tight budget. But you won't benefit if interest rates generally fall.

Loans secured on your home are normally cheaper than unsecured loans. But this means that if you can't keep up your payments, the lender can repossess your home to get the money you owe. It may not be worth the risk.

The best way to check the cost of paying by credit is to ask for a written quotation. Lenders must give written quotations if asked.

When deciding whether you can afford the monthly repayments, do not commit yourself up to the limit. Give yourself some leeway especially if it is a variable rate deal as the interest rate could rise. You also need money available to meet the unexpected.

You may be offered loan insurance which will add to the total cost of your credit, though you may be charged a lower interest rate. Look carefully at what you are offered. If you have suffered a medical condition in the past, or your company has shed labour recently, your claim may be rejected if you suffer ill health or are made redundant.

On the next page is a checklist of sensible credit

Table 1
GETTING THE RIGHT TYPE OF CREDIT

The relative cost of credit

Short term credit	**Medium term credit**	**Long term credit**
(A few weeks or mths)	(One to five years)	(Five years +)
LIKELY TO BE CHEAP		
Interest free credit	Personal loans	Secured loan from
Authorised overdrafts	Endowment loan	a bank or building
Credit cards	Credit Unions	society
LIKELY TO BE MOST EXPENSIVE		
Unauthorised overdrafts	Store credit	Credit brokers
Store cards	Credit brokers	

options for the short, medium and long term:

OVERDRAFTS

Avoid going into overdraft without permission. It is not so much the interest which is charged which makes this such a costly option but the extra fees you have to pay. Added together these have been known to push the APR up to the equivalent of 100 million per cent for borrowing less than £100 for a couple of weeks.

An agreed overdraft, on the other hand, could be your cheapest option if you only need to borrow for short periods. Work out how much you would like your overdraft limit to be and ask your bank. Don't ask for more than you need or can repay quickly otherwise your request may be refused. If you want to use this facility regularly, switch to a bank which has no fees and only charges you interest when you overdraw. Some banks give automatic free overdrafts of £20 or £100. (See also Gold Card overdrafts below.)

CREDIT CARDS

Credit cards have become one of the most popular forms of borrowing which is not surprising in view of their flexibility and convenience. Once your application is approved and a card issued, providing you stay within your credit limit and repay the minimum of 5%, or £5 if greater, of the amount owing every month, you can run up credit whenever you want to and pay it off as quickly or slowly as you wish.

If you settle your monthly account in full by the specified date, no interest will be charged. In this way, you can receive up to 56 days interest free credit between the date you make your purchase and the day you have to pay your bill. If the account is not cleared in full, however, interest will normally be charged from the date that you first made the transaction on your card.
There are now over 70 different credit cards in issue in the UK. With this growth has come more variety in the interest rates charged. Another major difference is that some charge an annual fee and others do not. An increasing range of perks are also being offered such as free travel accident insurance, free gifts, purchase protection, discounts on cars and motor club membership. There are also a wide range of affinity cards, where a donation is made to the organisation, charity or club of your choosing everytime you use the card.

Remember you are not restricted to taking a card from the bank where you have your current account, you can go to almost any bank or building society to get a credit card. Which one is right for you will depend on how you use your credit card:

If you always pay off your account in full, you should choose a card which does not have an annual fee. If you never pay interest, the rate of interest charged is immaterial. Look instead for the card which offers the sort of perks you would find most useful.

If you do not normally pay off your account in full, choose a card with a low rate of interest. This probably means you will be charged an annual fee but you will still normally be better off than with a card that does not have an annual fee but has a higher rate of interest.

If you sometimes do not pay off your account in full, the choice is not so straightforward. If it only happens once or twice a year, you will probably still be better off with a card that does not have an annual fee. If you pay interest more often, a card with a low rate of interest and an annual fee is likely to be the best choice. There are also some card providers which waive their annual fee if you spend more than, say, £2,000 p.a. on their card which are worth considering.

OTHER PLASTIC CARDS

Debit cards :
These cards work like cheques. There is no credit involved since the value of your purchase is deducted immediately from your bank account. These cards work like cheques. They are normally issued free-of-charge.

Charge cards:
These cards can be used like credit cards.

There is no limit on the amount you can spend but you must settle your account in full each month. There is normally a joining fee, as well as an annual fee for charge cards.

Gold cards:

These can be either credit cards or charge cards. They are only issued if you have an above average income. A high annual fee is often charged but holders get extra perks such as free insurance and free legal and medical helplines. With the gold charge cards, generous automatic overdraft facilities at favourable rates of interest are also available.

Store cards

These cards are issued by retailers and petrol stations. They normally function like ordinary credit cards, but they are often more expensive. They sometimes offer special perks such as shopping evenings and discounts but could discourage you from shopping around for cheaper bargains elsewhere. Best avoided unless you clear your bill every month.

PERSONAL LOANS

A good way of borrowing over the medium term is a personal loan from your bank or building society (building societies have been particularly competitive in this market in recent years). But if you are making a major purchase such as new furniture or new kitchen equipment, check first whether the retailer is offering interest free credit. If not, a personal loan is simple to arrange and if agreed you will receive cash or cheque immediately. If you get your loan in advance, you may be able to negotiate extra discounts from the retailer on the same basis as a cash buyer.

Personal loans of between £500 and £10,000 are normally available for terms of between one and five years. The interest rate is fixed until the end of the repayment term, so you know precisely what your payments will be. This will help you to budget and will save you money if interest rates rise during the term, but you won't benefit if rates fall. Some lenders penalise you by charging you one or two months extra interest if you pay off your loan early.

FINANCE COMPANY
LOANS AND HIRE
PURCHASE

Shops, car dealers and other suppliers of goods may offer to arrange a finance company loan or a hire purchase agreement if you are buying a large item. The cost of this type of credit varies considerably. It can be low cost but always check it against the cost of a bank loan. A bank loan may also give you an extra advantage because as a cash buyer you might be able to negotiate a discount.

Finance company loans work like bank loans but hire purchase agreements are quite different. As the name suggests, the goods you get through this type of agreement are effectively on hire until the final payment is made. So they remain the property of the seller and the borrower cannot sell them until the HP agreement is cleared.

You cannot cancel an HP agreement unless you are up to date with your payments and have paid at least half the amount owing. If you do cancel, the goods will have to be returned and the money you have already paid will be lost. But the seller cannot repossess the goods without a court order unless you give your permission.

Many car companies now offer their own credit deals which can be more attractive than bank loans. But car buyers need to look carefully. Some of these deals start off with low interest rates in the first year, but the rates shoot up thereafter. Another growing trend is Personal Contract Purchases (PCPs). These are expected to account for almost half of all car sales in the near future. PCP schemes come under a variety of names - Ford Options, Vauxhall 1-2-3, Rover Select Finance.

The way PCP schemes work is that when a car is purchased, the car company sets a guaranteed future value (GFV). This is the amount the car is expected to be worth at the end of the agreement, which is usually for two or three years. The GFV is deducted from the price of the car, minus your deposit, and repayments are based on this amount only. The interest, though, is calculated on the full price. So someone could buy a £12,000 car which has a GFV of £6,000 after three years and pay a 25% deposit. After the deposit, the buyer owes £9,000 (£12,000 less 25%). Instead of having to repay all of this, only £3,000 has to be repaid (£9,000 less the GFV of £6,000), plus interest on the whole £9,000. At the end of three years, £6,000 is still owed.

At the end of the three year agreement, the buyer has three choices. He can pay the outstanding amount and keep the car, return the car and pay no more (subject to satisfactory wear and tear and mileage), or sell the car and pay off the outstanding amount, keeping any profit on the sale over the GFV. With the last two options, he can buy a new car and start from the beginning again.

So how do PCPs compare with other types of credit? Because you are only paying for part of the car's value, the monthly repayments are usually a lot less than with a traditional HP agreement or bank loan which would cover the full cost of the car. But comparing costs in this way is somewhat misleading as you will still owe a substantial amount at the end of the PCP scheme.

PCPs are a low cost option if you want a new car every two or three years. Otherwise a bank loan may still work out cheaper in the long run.

ENDOWMENT POLICY LOANS

Using savings instead of borrowing may be a good idea but not if it means surrendering a with profits endowment policy. You will lose out if you cash in early. But you might be able to get a cheap loan from your insurance company, if your policy has been running several years, secured against the value of your policy. Interest rates on policy loans can be less than for personal loans or overdrafts. The loan is repaid from the payout when your policy reaches the end of its normal term and you may even be able to roll up the interest and pay it off at the end of the term too. However, if your policy is earmarked to pay off your mortgage then a loan will not be available.

SECURED LOANS

If you need to borrow over £10,000 or you want to spread loan repayments over the medium to long term, a loan secured on your home is often the cheapest way, providing you go to a reputable lender, such as your bank or a building society. They are normally prepared to lend providing your existing mortgage plus the loan required do not exceed 80%-90% of your current property value.

There are banks and building societies which offer secured loans on a 'second charge' basis (this means they are behind your existing lender in the repayment stakes). But try your existing mortgage lender first. They will normally be cheaper than going to another lender but they may restrict lending to such things as home improvements only. Look out for arrangement, valuation and legal fees with this sort of loan. Check what the penalties are if you think you may want to repay your loan early.

Remember you could lose your home if you default on payments. A lender with a 'second charge' can take you to court and demand repossession of your property even if you have kept your first lender happy.

CREDIT UNIONS

These are co-operative ventures set up by people with something in common - members of a club, church, estate. Members who save regularly for a certain period can get cheap loans. To find out if there is a credit union you can join or how to set one up contact the Association of British Credit Unions (0171 582 2626).

CREDIT BROKERS

Brokers often take out small ads in newspapers offering to lend to people already in debt. They suggest that the borrower will be better off clearing all other debts with a new loan. Don't be fooled. These loans are nearly always a lot more expensive in the long run. The broker who arranges the loan will get a large upfront fee. The loans often need to be secured on your property so there is the risk that you could lose it if you cannot keep up repayments. Even if you are desperate these loans should be avoided. It would be better to speak to your existing lenders, explain any problems you may have and ask if they could make your repayments more manageable.

ASSESSING YOUR
CREDITWORTHINESS
Lenders normally decide whether they will grant you credit or not by 'credit scoring' and/or consulting a credit reference agency.

Credit scoring
In order to find out whether you are a good credit risk, a lender may score you on the basis of the answers you give on your application form. A mark is given for various factors such as your job, your age and marital status. These scores vary according to each lender's experience, so different lenders can give different scores. The marks are added up and only those which are above that lender's 'pass mark' will be given credit. The lender is not obliged to tell you why you have been refused credit, but some will if you ask.

Credit reference agencies
Agencies collect factual information from the electoral roll, county court judgements, bankruptcies and other credit agreements. They do not give an opinion about you, they simply pass on the data to your prospective lender. If you ask, your lender is legally obliged to tell you which agency has been consulted.

If you want to see what information an agency holds on you, you must be sent a copy of your file providing you apply in writing, giving your full name, current address and any other address you've lived at during the previous six years, together with a £1 fee. The agency must reply within seven days. If you find any of the information is incorrect, you can ask for it to be corrected. The agency must send the correction to anyone who has consulted them about you in the past six months.

Debt problems often arise because of a change in circumstances - job loss, sickness, marital breakdown - which means there is not as much income available to keep up credit repayments. Check whether you have any insurance cover that may fill the breach. But in any case get in touch with your lenders and explain the situation. Tell them how much you can afford to pay. Make your mortgage or other secured loans your highest priority. Contact your local Citizens Advice Bureau or consumer advice centre for free help.

DEBT PROBLEMS

3   *Building up your capital*

Investment conditions are constantly changing. Interest rates rise and fall and so do share prices. But the key to successful investment remains the same. You need to aim for a happy balance between risk and reward by putting your money into a variety of different types of investments. This strategy holds true whether you can only afford to save a little each month or you have a lump sum to invest.

Besides getting your choice of investment products right, choosing the right company or investment manager to look after your money is equally important. Much attention nowadays tends to focus on charges, but this is only part of the equation. The strength of a company and its past performance record are also essential considerations.

It is also vital to keep your investments under regular review to make sure you are still getting the best results and be prepared to make changes if necessary. But don't let yourself be thrown off balance. Chasing the highest interest rates, the latest stockmarket fashion or the most generous tax breaks could lead you into the wrong investments.

To help you pick the right investments, there are four important questions you should ask yourself before you start saving or invest a lump sum.

Are my cash reserves adequate?

Always ensure you have a reserve fund in a secure, easily accessible account with a bank, building society or National Savings so that you have money available for emergencies. The amount should be equivalent to around three to six months regular outgoings. If you have a mortgage, make sure you have enough to bridge the gap until you can claim state help. Don't forget to top up your reserves if you need to dip into them.

When will I need the money?

If you are saving or investing capital for a particular purpose at a specific future date, make sure you can cash in your savings plan or investment at that time without penalty. If you do not know when you will need the money, make sure the investment scheme is flexible. But find out if there is a recommended minimum length of time you should leave your money invested to get best results.

How much risk is involved?

To get the highest rewards you often need to take high risks. So if an investment is offering high returns, find out whether you could lose money. Risk does not necessarily make an investment a bad idea but you don't want any nasty surprises. If you cannot afford to lose money, stick to low risk investments. But if you have money to invest longer term, you could get a better return by taking some risk.

Is this the most tax efficient investment for me?
Never choose an investment for tax reasons alone but once you have decided your objective it is sensible to seek out the most tax efficient investment to meet your needs.

MORE ABOUT RISK
AND REWARD

What is risk? In an investment context, risk refers to the possibility that you could lose money on your savings. The returns are usually commensurate with the amount of risk. You will normally receive higher returns from a high risk investment if all goes well - that's your reward for taking the extra risk. But if you are unlucky you could end up with less than you invested.

An example of a low risk investment is a building society account where you know your capital is safe and that you will get a steady flow of interest. Shares in a new company, on the other hand, represent the other end of the risk spectrum. You could lose everything if the company goes bust but if it does well your rewards can be very high.

When considering how much risk you are prepared to take, you should take time-scale into account. Share prices vary significantly over the short term and you could lose money if you want to cash in just as they fall. Money needed in the short term is better kept in low risk deposit accounts.

However stockmarkets recover and over longer terms shares have generally produced better returns than building society deposits. They have also performed better against inflation. Moreover you can reduce your risks by buying investments which hold a spread of shares, and therefore tend to vary less than the price of shares of an individual company.

Most investors would like to get the highest possible returns on their money without any risk. But finding a single investment which fulfils both requirements is impossible and any investment which makes such claims should be viewed with suspicion. The best approach is to build up a balanced portfolio of investments using a pyramid approach as follows:

GETTING A BALANCE BETWEEN RISK AND REWARD

1. Start by building the bottom of the pyramid with a solid foundation of low risk investments. These are investments that you can rely on through thick and thin. They will normally form the largest single element of your investment portfolio. They will include such things as building society deposits and National Savings products.

2. The next layer of the pyramid should consist of medium risk investments. Into this category would fit such things as with profits policies and Personal Equity Plans invested in unit or investment trusts with a broad investment spread.

3. Finally cap your pyramid with a small amount of higher risk investments. This is the stage at which to include some speculative investments - specialist unit or investment trusts, for example, or individual shares. As they only account for a small portion of your investments, if they go wrong it won't bring the whole pyramid down.

This pyramid strategy can be used for individual elements of your portfolio also. For example, if you want to build up your own share portfolio - start with the shares of solid, well known blue chip companies as your base, then smaller companies working up to, say, a speculative 'penny share' as your top brick so that if it becomes worthless you won't have lost very much.

GETTING THE BEST RETURNS

Besides getting the right mix of investments, you must also try to get the best returns from each of them. Many people do not give enough attention to this aspect and end up losing pounds as a result. While it is not always easy to predict which investment manager will achieve the best returns, you should at least rule out those whose track record is poor. Check regularly, say once a year, how competitive your returns are. If they have fallen behind, consider a switch. Many organisations rely on the apathy of their existing customers.

Never take the first offer that comes along, say from your bank, without checking how it compares with what other institutions can offer. The 'money' pages in your daily newspaper can be helpful in this respect. But to assist you further, sources of additional information and performance data, where applicable, will be given for each investment in this chapter so that you can get up-to-date comparisons.

CHARGES

Insurance companies must now disclose in money terms the commission paid to the financial adviser or sales person who recommends a product. They must show the effect of their charges on the likely returns and how much you will get back if you cash in early. A written explanation of why a product is suitable for your needs must also be given.

But don't invest with one company simply because it has lower charges than another. If it is an investment product, you must also weigh up each company's investment record. Lower charges cannot make up for poor investment performance. But good results can soon offset higher charges. So it may be worth paying more if you are likely to get better returns.

LOW RISK INVESTMENTS

A building society account is often the best place to put the first tranche of your savings and some bank accounts are worth considering too. But there are many different types of accounts on offer nowadays and interest rates vary widely so you will need to look around quite carefully to get the best deal. (See the end of this chapter for where to find up-to-date details on which societies are offering the best rates.)

BANK AND BUILDING
SOCIETY ACCOUNTS

If you have a lump sum to invest, remember that most societies now offer tiered rates of interest paying a higher rate the more you invest. So find out which society gives the best rate for the amount you have to invest and if you are marginally below a higher rate tier try to top it up if you can.

Consider postal accounts as they often pay higher rates and it only makes a few days difference when you want to withdraw money. Don't just stick to instant access accounts either. Make use of higher interest 30 to 60 day notice accounts. If you consider it unlikely that you will need all of your money at short notice, consider locking part of your money away in a fixed rate or escalator bond which guarantees an increasing interest rate. But always check out the early encashment conditions.

If you have only a small sum to invest, you will have to look harder. Some larger societies are no longer prepared to handle very small accounts of less than £100 or only give very poor rates of interest. You will often get the best rates of interest from smaller, localised societies. Look out for one in your vicinity, or ask about a postal account.

For details of which building societies and banks are paying the best rates, check your newspaper, or contact *Moneyfacts* (01692 500665).

TAX TIPS:

Make full use of tax free TESSAs - tax exempt special savings accounts (for more detail see below). If you are a non-taxpayer, don't forget to register the fact with your building society so you get your interest without tax deducted.

TESSAs

All bank and building society savers aged 18 or over should make full use of Tax-Exempt Special Savings Accounts (TESSAs) to earn tax free interest on their savings. You have to leave your money untouched for five years to qualify for tax free interest but you can withdraw your net interest during the term and you can get your savings back early if you need them. Even if you have to withdraw your savings early and pay tax on the interest, the returns on TESSAs are often more attractive than those offered on ordinary savings accounts for the same level of deposit.

You can start a TESSA with a lump sum or regular savings from as little as £1. The maximum lump sum deposit in the first year is £3,000 or £250 per month. In years two to five the maximum is £1,800 or £150 per month until you reach the maximum deposit of £9,000. You do not have to continue savings for the full term, though some TESSAs pay higher rates of interest if you subscribe the maximum amount.

After you have completed your first TESSA you will be able to open a second TESSA with the full amount of the capital deposited in your first TESSA, but not the accumulated interest.

The exact details of how each TESSA works, such as the rate of interest, whether it is fixed or variable and whether there are penalties on early withdrawal, varies from one bank or building society to the next. So it is important to shop around. If you find your TESSA has become uncompetitive, you can also switch it to a new provider without losing its tax free status.

To find out where you can get the best rates on TESSAs check your newspaper or contact *Moneyfacts* (01692 500665) or look in the magazine *Money Observer*.

NATIONAL SAVINGS

For smaller savers and money needed at short notice, the NS Ordinary and Investment Accounts can be competitive alternatives to bank and building society accounts. They are also convenient because they can be operated through any Post Office. The ordinary account is an instant access account which requires an opening balance of £10. The investment account can be started with £20, withdrawals require one month's notice. Interest on the accounts is taxable (except for the first £70 of interest on the ordinary account) but it is paid without tax deducted which is useful for non-taxpayers.

It is usually a good idea for everyone to own some NS Certificates because they give a guaranteed, Government-backed tax free return.

There are two types and amounts of between £100 and £10,000 can be invested in each. Fixed rate certificates pay a set rate of interest, which increases each year for five years. Index linked certificates pay a return in line with inflation as measured by the Retail Price Index, plus a fixed interest rate bonus on top. They are the easiest way of guaranteeing that your money is protected against erosion by inflation.

Withdrawals from NS Certificates can be made at any time, but best returns are achieved if you leave your money for the full five year term in each case. Don't forget to take action when your certificates reach maturity - switch to the current issue or an alternative investment.

If you don't want to commit yourself for five years, one year fixed rate FIRST Option Bonds are worth considering if you have a modest lump sum (minimum £1,000). It could give you a better return than a building society.

Don't forget Premium Bonds, they could make you a millionaire. The minimum stake is now £100, the maximum is £20,000. Besides the monthly £1m prize, there are smaller prizes ranging between £100,000 and £50. They are all tax free. Unlike the National Lottery, you can get your money back if you don't win. Withdrawals can be made at eight days' notice.

TAX TIP:
Remember the first £70 of annual interest is tax free on the NS Ordinary Account, the entitlement is doubled on a joint account.

CASH OR MONEY
MARKET FUNDS

These funds are offered by some unit trust companies. They pool investors' money and make bulk deposits with banks to gain top money market rates of interest. They can be an attractive alternative to building society accounts and some funds offer cheque book facilities. Interest rates can be competitive, especially for small amounts. Interest can be left to accumulate within the fund or paid out at regular intervals. Money can be withdrawn within a few days. Choose a fund with no up-front charge. Minimum investment starts at £500 and some funds have regular savings schemes starting at £25 a month. Interest is paid net of basic rate tax. Look in the press at the unit trust listings to see which funds are offering the best yields.

You may be offered one of these schemes by your employer. The object is to enable you to buy shares in the company you work for but in the initial savings period your money is simply put on deposit in a bank or building society so there is no risk. A fixed monthly amount is deducted from your pay for five years and you then receive a tax free bonus. If you leave your money a further two years you receive another bonus. At the end of these periods you can decide whether you want to buy the shares or not.

SAVE-AS-YOU-EARN SHARE OPTION SCHEMES

When you join a scheme you will be given the option to buy a fixed number of shares in your company at a fixed price. This may be the price at the time the scheme starts, or it could be less. Employers can give a discount of up to 20%. When the savings period ends, you do not have to buy the shares and, indeed, if their price has gone down, there would be no point in doing so because you could buy them cheaper through a stockbroker. If this happens, you can simply take the cash proceeds of the plan. If the price of the shares has risen you have a choice: you could buy them and resell them immediately at a profit. (No income tax is payable on this gain except with some old schemes); or if you decide to hold on to the shares, you could transfer them into a Personal Equity Plan in order to avoid future tax. If you do decide to retain the shares, this would become a higher risk investment as they will naturally fluctuate in price.

GILTS

The Government borrows money from the public and institutions through the sale of Gilt Edged Securities. Being Government backed, they are regarded as one of the safest of investments. They guarantee a fixed rate of interest, known as the 'coupon', and a fixed repayment of capital.

If you are investing for capital growth your main choices are Low Coupon Gilts or Index Linked Gilts. Low Coupon Gilts pay a lower rate of interest than the average gilt but they can be purchased at a discount and redeemed for their full value at maturity. Index Linked Gilts also pay only a modest income, though this is increased in line with inflation. The index linked capital gain on these stocks is only paid out by the Government at maturity but, in the meantime, its price will normally rise to reflect the underlying gains through the movement in the Retail Price Index.

You can sell gilts at any time but the price you get will depend on market conditions. To be sure of your return it is best to hold them to maturity. Choose a stock with a maturity date which suits your needs.

More details about gilts, how to buy them and how they can be used to provide a regular income are given in Chapter Four.

TAX TIP:
Capital gains from gilts are tax free.

These bonds are issued by insurance companies and pay a fixed rate of interest normally for terms of one to five years. Minimum investment starts at £1,000. Your capital plus interest is returned net of basic rate tax at the end of the period. They are a good way of adding an element of certainty to your investment returns and are especially attractive when interest rates are about to fall. But you have to be certain you won't need your money before maturity as early encashment may not be allowed or only on unattractive terms. Rates on these bonds change quickly so contact an independent financial adviser to find out which company is offering the best rates when you want to invest.

TAX TIP:
These bonds are not suitable for non-taxpayers as tax cannot be reclaimed.

These are a relatively new type of investment which are offered by banks, insurance companies and building societies. Lump sum investment starts at around £1,000. They provide a fixed percentage of the growth in a stockmarket index or your money back at the end of the period if the index has fallen. They are typically for a five year term. The guarantees don't apply if you cash in early. Most bonds link their returns to the FT-SE 100 share index, which measures movements in the share prices of Britain's largest 100 companies. Some bonds are available linked to overseas stockmarkets.

Look out for those bonds which offer a return on your capital even if the stockmarket falls over the period. Many bonds are issued in limited tranches so you will need to find out from an independent financial adviser what is on offer currently.

TAX TIP:
Taxpayers will usually be better off with an
insurance guaranteed equity bond, than one
from a building society where income tax is
payable on the whole gain at maturity.

MEDIUM RISK INVESTMENTS

WITH-PROFITS
ENDOWMENTS/BONDS

With-profits policies are now available to lump sum investors as well as regular savers. Lump sum investment normally starts at £2,000. Regular savings start from a minimum of around £25 a month. In each case your money is invested by the insurance company in a fund containing a mixture of property, shares and fixed interest securities. The profits it makes on these assets, and other business activities, are distributed to policyholders in the form of bonuses.

There are two types of bonuses - annual and terminal. Annual bonuses generally reflect the company's investment income and, in theory, once they are added to your policy they cannot be taken away. Insurance companies use these bonuses to try and smooth out fluctuations in the investment markets and provide steady growth. In the good years, some investment returns are held back to cushion the fall in bonuses when conditions are not so good. A terminal bonus may be added at the end of your policy to give you the benefit of rises in capital values during the period of your policy. The terminal bonuses are more likely to fluctuate from year to year, in line with investment markets.

With-profits endowments provide some life insurance. They run for fixed terms. The minimum is 10 years. They should not be surrendered early because you will not get full value for money. A better way of getting money from your policy is to find out if you can sell it 'second hand'. You may get more this way than by surrendering.

The payout you receive from an endowment is free of tax provided you hold it for at least ten years, or three quarters of its term, if less. A financial adviser can help you here.

You are not locked into a lump sum with profits bond for a fixed term. But there may be early surrender penalties if you want your cash back within three years. The recommended minimum term is usually five years, but most insurers still retain the right to make an unspecified 'market value adjustment' deduction in the event of adverse stockmarket conditions. (For details of how with-profits bonds are taxed see investment bonds below.)

Historically with-profits policies have produced better returns than building society accounts, without the volatility of a direct investment in shares. But returns are not guaranteed. For surveys of which insurance companies have achieved the best returns in the past and which are financially strong, look in the magazine *Money Management.*

TAX TIP:
Withdrawals of 5% p.a. can be made from with-profits bonds without any immediate liability to extra tax.

The attraction of these ten year savings plans is that any investment growth is tax free, though this advantage is offset by their relatively high charges. Getting past performance results is also tricky. The underlying investments and level of

TAX EXEMPT FRIENDLY
SOCIETY PLANS

risk varies from plan to plan. Some companies offer with profits or fixed interest plans, others are more risky share linked schemes. Because of the tax concessions, investors are only allowed one plan each and the maximum premiums are £270 a year or £25 a month. Lump sum schemes are also offered. A capital sum is used to buy an annuity which makes regular payments to fund the premiums (but these annuity payments are taxable). Early encashment of Friendly Society plans should be avoided since you will be penalised for early surrender.

NON-SPECIALIST UNIT TRUSTS

Unit trusts give you easy and cheap access to a professionally managed portfolio of fixed interest investments or shares. It means you get a wide spread of investments for relatively small lump sums starting from £500, or monthly savings of £30. This does not take all the risk out of investing in the stockmarket, since if there is a general fall in prices the value of your investments will fall also, but unit trusts reduce the risks substantially because you never have all your eggs in one basket.

Another advantage of investing through unit trusts rather than direct is that you don't have to worry about when to buy and sell - professional fund managers monitor investment trends day-by-day and make these decisions for you.

When you invest in a unit trust you are allotted a certain number of units at a given price, say 25p. The price of the units moves in line with the value of the underlying investments. You can follow the progress of your investment easily because unit trust prices are published in the press each day.

There are many different unit trusts to choose

from. Your first choices should be a fixed interest fund and then a general trust, such as a UK growth trust which invests in a variety of different companies' shares, and after that an international trust which spreads your investment across a number of countries. Other medium to lower risk choices include balanced trusts which hold a mixture of shares and fixed interest investments and international bond funds which invest in the overseas equivalents of gilts and corporate bonds.

A major attraction of unit trusts is their flexibility. You can save regularly in a unit trust but you are not committed to continuing for a fixed period. You can stop saving at any time and leave your money invested until you need it (providing you have built up the minimum lump sum required). Another advantage of saving plans is that you do not have to worry about getting the timing of your investment right. Because you will be buying units when the stockmarket goes down as well as when it goes up, you will buy more units and the average price of your units will be reduced. This is known as 'pound cost averaging'. When the market recovers, you will benefit from having more units.

You can withdraw money from a unit trust whenever you need it without penalty (though a few trusts have exit charges in the early years). But to get the best results you should normally aim to leave your money untouched for at least five years.

Any income which a unit trust generates has basic rate tax deducted. Any growth is liable to capital gains tax but only if it exceeds your annual capital gains tax exemption.

For more information about unit trusts contact the Association of Unit Trusts and Investment

Funds (0171 831 0898). For unit trust performance look in the magazines *Money Observer* or *Money Management.*

TAX TIP:
You can hold many unit trusts free of tax
within a Personal Equity Plan (PEP).
(For more detail see below.)

NON-SPECIALIST
INVESTMENT TRUSTS

Investment trusts are similar to unit trusts. They also provide professionally managed portfolios of shares and other investments. But there are some important differences. Investment trusts are companies in their own right. When you invest in them you buy their shares, the price of which depends largely on the value of their investments but is also affected by the demand for their shares. The price of the shares, therefore, does not always match the actual value of the trusts' investments. Sometimes they sell at a discount and sometimes at a premium. It is best not to buy a trust which is at a premium. Buying at a discount can be an advantage. In recent years, investment trust discounts have narrowed and this has given a boost to their performance.

For a medium risk investment, your first choice should normally be in a general international or UK trust. Most trusts have one type of share which give investors equal rights to any income and growth generated. But some are split capital trusts which have a fixed life and different types of shares. The lowest risk are the zero dividend preference shares which give you a fixed annual capital return. Capital shares of splits can provide even better growth but they are higher risk and you should seek professional advice before investing.

Investment trust shares can be bought at low

cost through the managers. Lump sum and regular savings schemes are available. Withdrawals can be made at any time without penalty, but it is best to leave money invested for at least five years. Investment trusts are taxed like unit trusts.

For more information about investment trusts contact the Association of Investment Trust Companies (0171 588 5347). Performance information can also be found in the magazines *Money Observer* and *Investment Trusts.*

TAX TIP:
Many investment trusts can be held free of tax in a Personal Equity Plan. Zero dividend preference shares in investment trusts can also provide tax free growth providing gains fall within your annual capital gains tax exemption.

PERSONAL
EQUITY PLANS

Through a general Personal Equity Plan (PEP) you can invest direct in shares and corporate bonds (the latter from April 1995), preference shares and convertibles as well as unit trusts and investment trusts. Any income or capital growth from these investments will be totally free of tax. You can put in lump sums starting from £500, or make regular savings from £30 per month. The maximum anyone can invest is £6,000 in any one tax year.

You are only allowed to invest with one PEP manager per year. You can invest the full £6,000 in one unit or investment trust providing it is 'qualifying', i.e. it has at least 50% of its investment in the UK or EC stockmarkets. Or, if permitted by the PEP manager, you can hold more than one trust which can include up to £1,500 invested in a non-qualifying trust which invests in other parts of the world.

Investors in PEPs must be aged 18 or over and be resident in the UK for tax purposes.

You can withdraw your money from a PEP at any time (though there may be an exit charge in the early years), but they should be regarded as five year investments.

Look carefully at unit and investment trust performance before you buy a trust through a PEP.

TAX TIP:
If you are dissatisfied with the performance of your PEP, don't cash it in because you will lose the tax benefits. You can transfer your investment to a new PEP manager and not lose the tax free status.

INVESTMENT BONDS

Investment bonds are issued by insurance companies. They offer a choice of funds investing in UK and overseas shares, property, fixed interest and cash deposits. Lowest risk and best for most investors, however, are managed funds which hold a mixture of investments.

Higher rate taxpayers can gain from bonds because the investment income is taxed as that of the life company at a maximum rate of 25% and rolls up within the bond until encashment. On unit trusts, the investor must pay his normal rate of tax on any income (unless held within a PEP).

On encashment of a bond, higher rate tax may be payable. But first any gain will be top-sliced which may help to reduce the tax bill. Top-slicing involves the gain, i.e. the difference between the bond's current value and its original purchase price, being divided by the number of years the bond has been held and the resulting 'slice' added to the bondholder's income in the year of encashment. The tax rate payable on that slice will determine the tax rate applicable to the whole gain.

Capital gains are taxed within the bond, though this is normally less than the full rate. For investors with substantial capital gains, bonds can be advantageous. But for basic rate tax payers, unit trusts are more tax efficient.

One advantage of investment bonds is that it is possible to switch between investment funds without incurring capital gains tax and at low cost. Switching funds close to retirement into a fixed-interest fund can be a useful way of consolidating gains.

Minimum investment in a bond usually starts at £1,000 and withdrawals can be made at any time but they are best regarded as a five year investment. To see how well different companies' investment funds perform look in the magazine *Money Management*.

TAX TIP:
If you are a higher rate taxpayer, try to leave encashment of your bond until your income is lower, such as after retirement so that extra tax can be avoided.

UNIT LINKED ENDOWMENTS

These are regular savings plans which include some life insurance and run for a minimum of ten years. You have a choice of different investment funds. The value of the policy will fluctuate in line with the value of the underlying investment fund. This means you get the full benefit of any gains, but you are not cushioned if the investment market falls as you are through a with-profits policy. You can minimise your risk by opting for a managed fund which invests in a spread of equity, property and fixed interest holdings.

Unless you need life cover, for example, you are using the policy for mortgage repayment, unit linked policies are best avoided nowadays. Personal Equity Plans or unit trust savings plans are lower cost and more tax efficient.

HIGH RISK INVESTMENTS

SPECIALIST UNIT AND
INVESTMENT TRUSTS

There are growing numbers of unit and investment trusts that specialise in certain types of shares or overseas stockmarkets. These are higher risk than the more general trusts and trusts that hold assets outside the UK involve an extra uncertainty because of exchange rate movements.

Examples of those which specialise by type of share include smaller companies trusts, commodity trusts and property trusts. Overseas invested trusts include those investing in major world markets such as the United States, Europe and Japan and those which specialise on the smaller stockmarkets in the Far East and Latin America - the so-called Emerging Economies.

For more details about trusts see sections on non-specialist unit and investment trusts above.

SHARES

Direct investment in shares has become increasingly popular in recent years as a result of the Government's privatisations of companies, such as British Telecom, British Gas and the water authorities, in which shares were offered to the public at prices virtually guaranteed to ensure profit.

Any individual share is high risk because you are dependent on the fortunes of just one company. However, different types of shares involve different amounts of risk. Shares in large well established companies are far less risky than those of smaller companies which do not have much of a track record. The returns you can expect from different shares will reflect this difference.

Shares of large blue chip companies will not be so volatile. You won't see enormous jumps in their prices but you are less likely to lose your shirt. At the other end of the risk scale are shares of smaller companies. They can be very volatile. You could see the value of your shares rocket if the company is successful or they could become worthless if the company goes bust.

In some instances a small direct holding in a share may be advantageous because of the perks that are offered to shareholders such as discounts on the company's products or services.

It is now much easier to buy shares through building societies and banks if you know what you want. There are also telephone dealing services. These services are relatively cheap but if you want advice you will need to go to a stockbroker.

The minimum amount to invest in shares is determined by practical considerations. Because you will have to pay commission when you buy and sell your shares, this could wipe out your gains if you have only made a modest investment. The recommended minimum per share is usually £1,000 to £5,000. If you want to build a portfolio you should aim to invest in at least 10 to 15 shares. If you want a stockbroker to manage a share portfolio on your behalf you will usually need at least £50,000.

Share dividends are paid net of basic rate tax. Gains are subject to capital gains tax if you exceed your annual capital gains tax exemption.

For more information on investing in shares and stockbrokers, contact ProShare (0171 600 0984). Magazines such as *Money Observer* and the *Investors Chronicle* discuss the prospects for individual companies. Stockbrokers such as Sharelink also offer lists of recommended shares.

TAX TIP:
You can choose and hold your own shares
through a self select PEP and your returns will
be tax free.

SINGLE COMPANY OR CORPORATE PEPs

You can invest £3,000 p.a. in a single company PEP so that any income and gains are tax free. If £3,000 is a large portion of your savings this is a high risk strategy because it means you are putting too many eggs in one basket.

Some companies offer their shareholders a general corporate PEP. These are cost efficient but can be restrictive as you can normally only invest in that one company's shares. They must also be regarded as high risk because if the company suffers a set back, your whole PEP will suffer.

SHARE OPTIONS

Options give you the right to buy or sell shares for a given price within a fixed period. If you know what you are doing you can use them to profit from falls as well as increases in the stockmarket. But you can end up losing the cost of the option.

For a free information pack contact the London Financial Futures and Options Exchange (0171 379 2486).

Enterprise Investment Schemes have replaced Business Expansion Schemes. Designed to encourage investors to put money into small business, the EIS allows you to buy up to £100,000 of shares in qualifying unquoted trading companies per tax year and receive income tax relief of 20%. In addition you can invest the proceeds from the sale of other investments and defer any liability to capital gains tax on this money so you may qualify for total initial tax relief of up to 60%.

ENTERPRISE INVESTMENT SCHEMES

Providing you hold your shares acquired through the EIS for five years you will not be liable to tax on any dividends or capital gains received on the shares when you sell them. But bear in mind these are very high risk schemes since unquoted companies have a greater tendency to go bust than quoted companies. It will be somewhat less risky to invest through a Venture Capital Trust.

These are investment trusts which must invest most of their assets in small unquoted companies. Investors in the trusts will be entitled to income tax relief at 20% on investments up to £100,000 in any tax year providing that the shares are held for at least five years. Investors will also be able to invest the proceeds of other investments and defer liability to capital gains tax on this money so an investor can qualify for

VENTURE CAPITAL TRUSTS

total relief of up to 60%, as with EIS.

Any dividends and capital gains on VCT shares will be free of tax. As the trusts will invest in a number of different companies, they will be lower risk than the EIS but there is still a much higher chance of losing money than in an ordinary investment trust.

ALTERNATIVE INVESTMENTS

It is possible to regard objects such as gold coins, diamonds, wine, stamps or antiques as investments. But they are certainly in the high risk category since their worth often depends on totally unpredictable factors such as fashion and they generate no income. However, if you get enjoyment out of owning such assets anyway, in addition to regarding them as investments, you may well feel that the risk is worth taking because you will get some benefit regardless of what happens to their price.

MEMBERSHIP OF LLOYDS

To become a member of Lloyds you must be able to show ownership of readily realisable assets of at least £250,000. However, nowadays there are other ways of participating in Lloyds, such as through specialist investment trusts with a modest investment of as little as £250 which could still bring you above average rewards without the traditionally very high level of risk.

In the past, becoming a member of Lloyds represented the ultimate risk investment because you had to accept unlimited liability. The attraction was that you could make your capital work twice over. Firstly, you could receive the usual returns from the shares or other investment you held. Secondly the capital could be used to support the underwriting of insurance risks through syndicates at Lloyds in order to receive profits from that underwriting activity. But if an insurance claim was made you had to be prepared to sacrifice that capital and all the rest of your worldly wealth as well.

However, the extreme hardship this rule has caused to some members in recent years has led to liability being restricted to 80% of total premium income being written over a four year period. But this could still mean a major sacrifice. By taking a stake in a specialist Lloyds investment trust, you can restrict your loss to no more than your original investment.

OFFSHORE INVESTMENTS

A variety of investments are offered to UK residents by companies based outside the UK, for example, in the Channel Islands, Ireland and Luxembourg. They range from offshore bank and building society accounts to equity investment funds. They can offer tax advantages - though you cannot avoid tax on any income or gains remitted to the UK, you may be able to defer tax by putting money offshore. But always be sure to check out an offshore institution carefully before making an investment as you may not have the same level of protection or safety net of a compensation scheme if anything goes wrong as you would in the UK. If the parent company is a solid, mainstream UK institution, however, you have little to worry about.

Overleaf is a table showing how various investments have performed in the past.

HOW VARIOUS INVESTMENTS HAVE PERFORMED IN THE PAST

Value of £1,000 invested over different periods

	1 year £	5 years £	10 years £
Bank account	1004	1082	1354
Building Society	1028	1323	1921
National Savings Certificates			
Fixed Rate	1040	1436	1828
Index Linked	1039	1496	2263
Gilts			
(FT All Stocks)	954	1566	2198
Unit Trusts			
(Average UK General)	943	1349	3175
Average PEP Qualifying Unit Trust	1022	1528	4067
Investment Trusts			
(Average International General)	1047	1758	4358
FTSE 100 shares	973	1353	2609
Inflation (Retail Price Index)	1025	1225	1597

All figures to 1.12.94
Source: Micropal, Dept of National Savings

4   *Maximising your investment income*

The time most people need to invest a lump sum for income is when they reach retirement. Until then your first priority is usually to build up capital through savings and growth. But if you have been made redundant you may also need an income from your savings to help you bridge the gap between jobs.

If you have been made redundant, you will need to take a different approach to income investment than someone who has retired. You should keep all your money in low risk, easy access investments. Do not lock it away in long term investments such as insurance bonds. You may need to dip into your capital and you will be penalised if you have to cash in such an investment early. Also when you get back to work and no longer need extra income, you will need to revise your investments.

If you have retired, however, or your redundancy has brought about your early retirement, you will need to adopt a longer term approach. As more people retire early and live longer, it is not uncommon for retirement to last twenty years or more. You need to bear this in mind when you are deciding where to invest. It is important not to rush into any decisions. When you first retire you should wait a while before working out how much income you really need. It may take you a time to adjust to your new life. When you have calculated your income requirements, Table 1 will show you what interest rate or yield you need to achieve on your savings to get the right income. But if possible, try not to invest for maximum income to start with. Try to put some money aside for growth, such as in a unit or investment trust Personal Equity Plan, so you will have some extra money to invest for income later. Bear in mind also that your needs will change during retirement so you will need to keep your options open. Don't lock everything into long term plans.

Table 1

INCOME READY RECKONER - HOW MUCH INCOME YOU WOULD GET FROM YOUR CAPITAL AT DIFFERENT INTEREST RATES?

Annual income, before and after basic rate tax (at 25%), at different interest rates/yields

Amount invested	4% £ Gross	£ Net	6% £ Gross	£ Net	8% £ Gross	£ Net	10% £ Gross	£ Net
£5,000	200	150	300	225	400	300	500	375
£10,000	400	300	600	450	800	600	1000	750
£20,000	800	600	1200	900	1600	1200	2000	1500
£50,000	2000	1500	3000	2250	4000	3000	5000	3750

THE EQUITY INCOME STORY (PART 1)

Annual income earned from £1,000 lump sum invested in the average UK Equity Income unit trust compared to the net interest earned on a Building Society account over 10 years to 1st November 1994

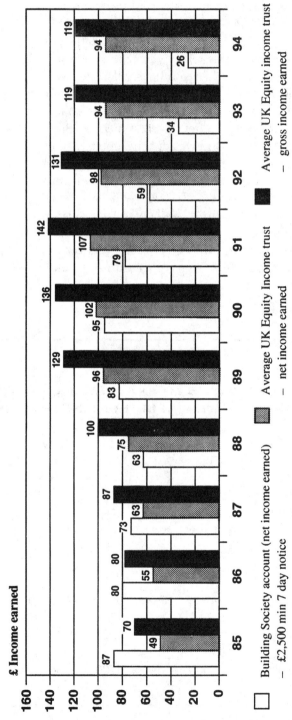

£ Income earned

Building Society account (net income earned) – £2,500 min 7 day notice

Average UK Equity Income trust – net income earned

Average UK Equity income trust – gross income earned

Figures on an offer to bid basis

Source: Hindsight from HSW, Micropal

THE EQUITY INCOME STORY (PART II)

Capital Growth of £1,000 lump sum invested in the average
UK Equity Income unit trust compared to a Building Society account
(income withdrawn) over 10 years to 1st November 1994

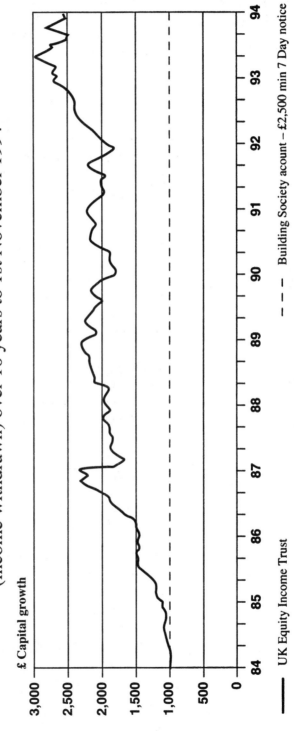

——— UK Equity Income Trust

– – – Building Society acount – £2,500 min 7 Day notice

Figures on an offer to bid basis

Source: Hindsight from HSW, Micropal

HOW TO CREATE AN INCOME PORTFOLIO

One clear lesson of the last twenty years for anyone who is investing for income is that you should not rely on any one source of income alone. People who relied on building society interest, for example, have been hard hit. During the 1970s and 1980s, they saw their income eroded by inflation and during the early 1990s interest rates fell sharply. Nevertheless, investment security is very important if you are relying on your capital to provide income. You cannot afford to take any unnecessary risks. So low risk investments are likely to form the majority of your investment portfolio.

However, some exposure to share linked investments should be included if possible. In the past, over periods of five to ten years, income from shares has exceeded returns from building society or fixed interest investment and shares can also help to protect your capital from being reduced in value by inflation. This is illustrated in Table 2 which compares returns from the average UK Equity Income unit trust with the net interest on a building society account. But no more than a quarter to a third of your money should be put into share linked investments - however good the returns may appear - because of the risk of losing money.

You will also be faced with choosing between investments which pay a fixed or variable income. A fixed income is attractive because it makes budgeting easier but there can be snags. With some investments it means you miss out if interest rates go up. Other products use your capital to top up the fixed 'income'. Nevertheless a mixture of fixed and variable rate investments can be a good idea.

Table 3 gives you an at-a-glance menu from which you can pick and mix. The sections below give you more detail.

Table 3
INCOME CHOICES

Low Risk	Medium Risk	Higher Risk
Building societies*	Unit trust PEPs	Guaranteed Equity
TESSAs	Investment trust PEPs	Income Bonds#
National Savings*	With profits bonds#	Shares
Cash funds	Distributions bonds#	Income Shares of
Guaranteed Income	Corporate bonds*	Investment trusts
Bonds*	Annuity investment plans*	
Gilts*		
PIBS*		
Annuities*		

*Fixed income available
#Fixed income available but beware of capital erosion.

Look out for the investments which will provide you with the most tax efficient income. Which investments suit you best will depend on your own tax position - whether you are a non taxpayer, a basic rate taxpayer or higher rate taxpayer, or whether you could fall into the 'age allowance trap' and lose your extra tax allowance if you are aged over 65 (this problem is discussed in more detail in Chapter 5). Tax will be discussed in the context of each of the main income investments below.

If you are married, you should make sure that you and your spouse have divided your assets in order to take advantage of independent taxation since this could also help to reduce the tax you pay on your income. (Independent taxation is also discussed in more detail in Chapter 5.)

TAX

THE MAIN INCOME INVESTMENTS

BANKS AND BUILDING
SOCIETIES

All investors need to keep some money easily available in a bank or building society savings account to meet unexpected expenses. But you should not keep all of this reserve fund in an instant access account. A 30 or 90 day account will give you a higher rate of interest and you can still get at the money easily enough if you need it, though you may have to pay an interest rate penalty. Most societies offer a monthly income facility on such accounts and will transfer this money into a current account automatically on your behalf. Postal accounts often provide the most competitive rates and also offer monthly income options.

The next tranche of your savings can also stay in a building society account. But this part does not have to be easily accessible. So use your TESSA allowance to save tax (see below) and other longer term accounts which offer monthly income facilities. Consider a fixed rate or escalator bond which pays a rising rate of interest, usually over five years. But don't lock into such a bond if there is a possibility of general interest rate rise in the near future.

Interest on building society and bank accounts is usually paid net of basic rate tax but if you are a non-taxpayer you can obtain it without tax deducted.

For the best building society accounts contact *Moneyfacts* (01692 500665).

TAX TIPS:
If your income falls into the 20% bracket, remember to claim back the extra tax deducted from your building society savings account. Make full use of TESSAs.

Tax exempt special savings accounts (TESSAs) offered by banks and building societies enable you to earn interest on your savings free of tax, providing your deposit is left untouched for a five year term. However, you can withdraw the interest less tax during the term, and some banks and building societies offer monthly income facilities on their TESSAs for this purpose. At the end of the term, you will then receive your capital plus the balance of the interest.

TESSAS

You can invest a maximum of £9,000 in a TESSA over five years starting with up to £3,000 in the first year, and then up to £1,800 in years two to five until you reach the maximum. If you have taken out a TESSA in the past you can roll over your capital (but not the interest) for a further five years and continue receiving tax free interest. If your existing TESSA does not provide monthly income, you can transfer it to another bank or building society without losing its tax free status, although your old provider may make a charge.

TAX TIP:
Even if you are unable to leave your savings for the full five years a TESSA may be worthwhile, since the interest rates after tax are often very competitive for the sums involved.

The National Savings Income Bond is a popular choice if you want a regular monthly income. The interest rate is variable but tends to fluctuate less than building society rates. It is usually competitive for smaller sums but always compare what the building societies have to offer first. Between £2,000 and £250,000 can be invested per person.

NATIONAL SAVINGS

A fixed income over five years is paid by the

Pensioners Guaranteed Income Bond which is available to people aged 65 and over. Amounts of between £500 and £20,000 can be invested.

Although National Savings Certificates do not pay an income, they are worth considering because returns are tax free and you can cash them in small quantities to provide the equivalent of an income. Interest is fixed for five years. Index Linked National Savings Certificates do not pay income either, but it is highly advisable to include some among your investments so that you have some guaranteed protection against inflation. Currently between £100 and £10,000 can be invested in both fixed rate and index linked certificates.

TAX TIP:
Interest on Income Bonds and Pensioners Guaranteed Income Bonds is paid without tax deducted, but is taxable. Remember to set money aside to pay the tax if a taxpayer.

CASH FUNDS

Cash funds can be a competitive alternative to a building society account for small amounts. They are unit trusts which pool investors' money and place it on deposit with banks at money market interest rates. (For more details see Chapter 3.) Payments of interest may be made half yearly, quarterly or monthly depending on the fund chosen. It is paid with basic rate tax deducted but this can be reclaimed if you are a basic rate taxpayer.

GILTS

Like National Savings, gilts provide a high level of security as they are issued by the Government. They pay a fixed income and a fixed capital return if they are held to maturity. Each stock has a different maturity date and they are usually grouped into short dated stocks with five years or less to redemption, medium dated with five to fifteen years to run and longer dated stocks. Private investors are normally recommended to opt for medium dated stocks.

Gilts are traded on the Stock Exchange like shares and can be purchased either through a stockbroker or through the National Savings Stock Register via the Post Office. The NSSR is the cheapest route - investing £1,000 via the NSSR will only cost you £6, but if you want advice on which stocks to buy you will need to ask a stockbroker. The cost of buying through a stockbroker will be £20-£30 minimum per stock.

Gilts are sold in £100 lots but the price you pay is rarely £100. Depending on demand and supply, you will either pay less which means you will receive a gain on maturity, or you pay a higher price which means you will make a loss if you hold the stock to maturity. It may be worth paying more for the income but it does mean the return you receive on your money will be less from the rate in the stock name - the so-called coupon. Similarly, if you buy at a discount the rate will be higher. For example, ignoring investment costs, if Treasury 8% 2006 is selling at £94.12, for example, it means you will actually receive a running yield of 8.5%. Adding the capital gain at maturity will boost your total return to the equivalent of 8.7%.

The price of gilts varies according to the general outlook for interest rates. So if you sell a gilt before it reaches maturity there is no guarantee how much you will get back.

Income from gilts is paid half yearly. The payment months are listed in the NSSR leaflet obtainable at main Post Offices. You can spread your investment across a number of gilts if you wish to receive a more frequent income. If you buy gilts through the NSSR, income is paid without tax deducted, otherwise it is paid net of basic rate tax.

Another option is to buy a unit trust which specialises in gilts. Managers aim to get the best income returns and some capital gains as well by trading between different stocks. Often they combine the gilts with other fixed interest stock such as corporate bonds in order to boost the returns.

TAX TIP:
Capital gains on gilts are tax free.

PIBS

Permanent Interest Bearing Securities (PIBS) are issued by building societies. They pay a fixed half yearly income but, unlike gilts, they have no maturity date so there is no fixed capital return. They are traded on the stock market so you will need to invest through a stockbroker.

CORPORATE BONDS,
PREFERENCE SHARES,
CONVERTIBLES

These are issued by companies which want to raise extra capital. They pay a fixed rate of interest. Corporate bonds have a fixed repayment date. The safest are debentures secured on specific company assets. Next for repayment if a company goes bust is unsecured loan stock. Preference shares do not have a fixed life but if something happens to a company they do rank ahead of ordinary shareholders for repayment. Convertibles give the holder the right to convert their holdings to ordinary shares at a fixed price during a fixed period, or receive repayment.

These stock pay higher rates of return than gilts, but are more risky. You need to get advice from a stockbroker or invest through a unit trust. Interest is paid net of basic rate tax.

TAX TIP:
Income and capital gains can be obtained tax
free on all of these investments if investment
takes place via a Personal Equity Plan.

These bonds pay a fixed income on a yearly, half yearly or monthly basis for a fixed period, typically of between one and five years. At the end of the term you get back your original capital. They are issued by insurance companies and should not be confused with the guaranteed equity income bonds where your capital is not guaranteed.

GUARANTEED
INCOME BONDS

The advantage of guaranteed income bonds is that they are easy to buy, you know what you are going to get and there are no additional buying or selling costs other than the internal charges. But compare the rates being offered with those available on building societies' fixed rate accounts.

Getting your capital back before the end of the term, however, may not be allowed or you may be penalised. Tax is paid by the insurance company and basic rate taxpayers will have no further tax to pay on the income. But higher rate taxpayers may face a higher rate charge if income exceeds 5% and on maturity.

TAX TIP:
Income bonds are not suitable for non-
taxpayers. Age allowance may also be affected
in the year the bond matures (see Chapter 5).

A higher than average 'income' is offered on these bonds which are normally sold by insurance companies, but they are effectively using your capital to provide this 'income'. At

GUARANTEED EQUITY
'INCOME' BONDS

the end of the term, typically five years, you will receive your original investment back only if the stockmarket has behaved as assumed under the bond conditions - normally it must have risen by a given percentage. If not, you could lose a large part of your capital. Most of these bonds are high risk and should be avoided if possible.

ANNUITIES

Annuities are one of the oldest forms of income investment available. They are sold by insurance companies and pay a guaranteed income which is partly determined by general interest rates and partly by your age and sex. Part of the income is tax free as it is regarded as a return of capital. The best time to buy is when interest rates are high because you can lock into those high rates.

The older you are the more income you get from an annuity, and men get a higher income than women of the same age, because men have shorter life expectancies. Annuity rates also differ considerably between insurance companies. To get the best possible income you will need the help of an independent financial adviser.

The advantage of lifetime annuities is that you know, come what may, you will always have an income - your capital won't run out. The main drawback is that the income is normally fixed so, while it may be quite adequate to start with, over the years it will be gradually eroded in value by inflation.

Possible solutions are to opt for annuities which rise by a fixed percentage each year, say 3% or 5%, or in line with the Retail Price Index. Unit linked and with profits annuities are also available where payments are likely to improve in line with investment performance. However, the problem with these annuities is that the payments normally start lower than with a level annuity and can take some time before they overtake them. For this reason it may be better to use part of your capital to buy the maximum level annuity first and then buy further annuities later to top up your income, when you will not only benefit from higher rates because you are older but also from a higher tax free capital element.

Another snag with immediate annuities is that once you hand over your capital you cannot get it back again. Your beneficiaries will miss out too, though it is possible to buy guaranteed or capital protected annuities so that some money is paid even after your death. There are also annuity investment schemes which package together an annuity and an investment product so that you get some capital back.

Under one type of scheme known as a back-to-back plan you invest your capital in a ten year temporary annuity. This provides fixed payments which provide an income and pay the premiums on an endowment or whole life insurance policy. The endowment is designed to grow sufficiently to provide you with a sum equivalent to your initial capital investment at the end of ten years, but this is not guaranteed. A whole life policy can be used to give your beneficiaries a capital sum when you die.

Shorter term schemes are also available where your capital is divided between a five year temporary annuity and a unit trust or investment bond (see below for more details on these products). Once again the temporary annuity provides you with an income, while the capital invested in the unit trust or investment bond is expected to grow to a sum equal to your initial investment - but this is not guaranteed.

TAX TIP:
Only part of the income from an annuity is
taxable. The remainder is treated as a return of
capital. The capital element varies with your
age and sex.

PERSONAL
EQUITY PLANS

You can receive a tax free income from shares and corporate bonds (after April 1995) by investing through a PEP. In order to keep risk to the minimum it is advisable to invest through a unit trust or investment trust PEP, which will give you a broad spread of investments even for a small sum. Investing direct in shares is a higher risk strategy unless you have enough capital to build up a diversified portfolio. However, if you still own shares from privatised companies which are relatively low risk, it is worth switching them into a single company or corporate PEP in order to get the dividends tax free. You can invest up to £6,000 p.a. in a unit or investment trust PEP starting with amounts from £500 or regular monthly savings of £30. For married couples the investment limit is doubled to £12,000.

UNIT TRUST PEPS

There are a number of different types of unit trusts designed to produce income which can be included within a PEP. Most pay out income half yearly, but some provide quarterly or monthly payments. The main trust categories are the 'UK Equity Income' trusts which invest in shares, the 'Fixed Interest' trusts which invest in corporate bonds, preference shares and convertibles, and the 'Balanced' trusts which combine shares and fixed interest investments.
It is important not to judge the relative merits of these trusts simply on the level of income they offer. Fixed Interest trusts will tend to have the largest yields and offer a relatively high level of security, but any growth in income or capital

will be modest. Equity Income trusts will usually have a more modest income to begin with but offer most scope for growth in their income and capital. Past experience indicates that after a few years the returns you get from this type of trust will comfortably exceed those from fixed interest trusts. Balanced trusts aim for a mixture of a high immediate return coupled with some growth.

Before investing in a unit trust check out its performance figures in magazines such as *Money Management* or *Money Observer*. If it is a new trust, look at how other trusts managed by the same company have performed.

INVESTMENT TRUST PEPS

It is even more important that income yields alone should not be used as a means of choosing a suitable investment trust. Most income producing investment trusts invest in shares and have a good past record for providing investors with a rising income and capital growth. A few include some fixed interest securities in their portfolios to give a boost to their yields.

But the highest incomes are provided by the special income shares of split capital trusts. These shares attract all the income from a trust's assets but not the capital growth. This can mean that your investment drops in value when the trust is wound up. You should seek professional advice before investing in income shares. For more information and performance tables look in *Investment Trusts* magazine or contact the Association of Investment Trust Companies (0171 588 5347).

Most investment bonds offered by insurance companies are designed primarily to produce capital growth but two types which are aimed at income investors are with-profits and distribution bonds. Both are regarded as reasonably low risk because they are not invested purely in shares.

**WITH-PROFITS AND
DISTRIBUTION BONDS**

With-profits bonds give investors a spread of shares, fixed interest and property investment. But what makes them different from other types of investment is the bonus system. The insurance company gives investors a share in the investment profits in the form of an annual bonus. Bonuses are used to smooth out fluctuations in investment returns - some profits are held back when markets are good to help to cushion the fall in bonus rates when conditions deteriorate. A terminal bonus may be added when the bond is cashed, or there may be a deduction if investment conditions are adverse.

Distribution bonds normally invest in a mixture of high yielding shares and fixed interest securities. The aim is to generate a high income with some prospect of capital growth, while maintaining a reasonable level of security. Regular payments can be taken from both types of bonds. Investors may be given the choice of how much income they wish to draw, though this freedom should be used with caution or you could start eating into your capital. There is no basic rate tax to pay on these withdrawals. An attraction for higher rate taxpayers or older investors who may be facing the age allowance trap - when their income is high enough to lead to a reduction in their personal allowance - is that 5% withdrawals can be made from a bond each year for up to 20 years without incurring any immediate tax liability. This 5% withdrawal is not treated as income for the calculation of the age allowance.

**RAISING AN INCOME
FROM YOUR HOME**

Many people find that when they get to retirement most of their capital is tied up in their home. A way of unlocking it without having to sell up and move to a smaller property is to use a home income plan. Although there has been some bad publicity about these plans in recent years, this related to one sort of plan that had been marketed in the late 1980s and has since been banned. Other safer schemes exist that have proved of considerable value to elderly home owners over the years.

These schemes combine a special fixed rate mortgage and an annuity. The company provides you with a loan up to 80% of the market value of your property which is used to purchase an annuity. The annuity payments provide enough money to pay the interest on the mortgage loan, net of basic rate tax relief, and the remainder gives the homeowner an extra income for life. The loan itself is not repayable until you die and can often be transferred to another property if you move. If the price of your property goes up you can go back to the lender and ask for a further loan to buy another annuity in order to increase your income.

MORTGAGE-BASED PLANS

Since home income schemes involve annuities, age is an important factor. Indeed, you normally have to be at least 70 for the income produced to be worthwhile, while married couples need to have reached a combined age of at least 150.

Another type of scheme for getting income from your home is known as a home reversion scheme. This involves selling your property to the company, rather than raising a mortgage, but retaining the right to live there for the rest of your life. The major attraction of the scheme is not having to worry about mortgage payments, you can keep all the annuity payments as your income. So you tend to get a better income than under a mortgage plan. You may be able to take a partial reversion and retain an interest in the house if you do not want to sell it outright. Always make sure you discuss your plans to take out a home income plan with your relatives before going ahead and take legal advice.

HOME REVERSION SCHEMES

5   *Beating the taxman*

T ax has become an increasing burden in recent years. Nobody likes paying more tax than they need to. Yet many people overlook ways in which they can save tax such as by arranging their affairs more tax efficiently, making full use of allowances or claiming back tax that may have been overpaid.

From 1996, self-assessment of taxation will be introduced (for people who start up in business some of the new rules already apply). The Inland Revenue has said that the new system will make things simpler and easier to understand. It will certainly make it even more important for all of us to become more aware of our tax affairs.

HOW YOU ARE TAXED

Before going on to look at specific areas where you may be able to make tax savings, here is a brief reminder of how your income and savings are taxed each year and some of the main pointers for tax planning.

Remember that a tax year runs from 6 April one year to 5 April the next. The amount of the allowances and tax bands for each year are often changed in the Government's annual Budget, and sometimes there are changes to the tax rates as well. Current rates are shown in Table 1.

Everybody gets a basic personal allowance.

This is the amount of income you can get free of tax each year. If all your income falls into this bracket, you are a non-taxpayer. When you reach 65 you qualify for a higher age related allowance, and at age 75 this age allowance is increased. Blind people get an extra tax allowance.

Tax planning: Make sure maximum use is being made of personal allowances. If receiving age allowance, make sure your income does not go over the limit.

All your other income is taxable.

However, married couples get an extra allowance on top of their basic personal allowance to offset against their tax bill. This allowance normally goes to the husband. Similar allowances are given to single parents and to widows for one or two years. A higher married couple's allowance is paid if one partner is aged 65 or over.

Tax planning: Check that the married couple's allowance is used to best effect.

Tax rates:

On the first slice of your taxable income you pay income tax at the rate of **20%**. The next part is taxed at the basic rate of income tax which is **25%**. Any further income is taxed at the higher rate of **40%**.

Tax planning: Check for ways of reducing income tax liabilities. Make full use of tax efficient investments.

Capital gains:

Each year you can take some capital gains on

your savings and investments free of tax, thereafter they become taxable. To work out the rate of tax you must pay, your taxable gains are added to your taxable income and taxed according to the income tax rate band into which they fall.

Tax planning: Make use of your annual capital gains tax exemption.

Inheritance tax:

No inheritance tax is payable on estates up to certain limits, but if they are worth more any excess will be taxed at 40%.

Tax planning: Make full use of inheritance tax exemptions.

Table 1
PERSONAL ALLOWANCES

	1994-95	1995-96
Personal allowance		
Under 65	£3,445	£3,525
65-74	£4,200	£4,630
75 or over	£4,370	£4,800
Blind Person's allowance	£1,200	£1,200
Married couple's allowance		
Both under 65	£1,720	£1,720
One partner 65-74	£2,665	£2,995
One partner 75 or over	£2,705	£3,035
Single parent allowance	£1,720	£1,720
Widow's bereavement allowance	£1,720	£1,720

Relief is 20% for 1994/95 and 15% for 1995/96

Table 2
RATES OF INCOME TAX

	Rate	1994/95 Taxable Income	1995/96 Taxable Income
Lower rate band	20%	£0-3,000	£0-3,200
Basic rate band	25%	£3,001-23,700	£3,201-24,300
Higher rate band	40%	£23,701+	£24,301+

CAPITAL GAINS TAX

	1994/95	1995/96
Annual Exemption	£5,800	£6,000

INHERITANCE TAX

Rate on excess	1994/95 Estate over	1995/96 Estate over
40%	£150,000	£154,000

TAX AND MARRIAGE

Since the introduction of independent taxation in 1990, when a married woman's income ceased to be treated as her husband's, there has been increased scope for couples to save tax. Opportunities arise principally when one partner is a non-taxpayer or pays a lower rate of tax than the other.

The married couple's allowance normally goes to the husband but a wife may choose to receive half the allowance, or, if both husband and wife agree, the whole allowance can go to the wife. It will save tax to transfer this allowance to a wife if her income is sufficient to claim the allowance, and her husband is a non-taxpayer or is earning less than the allowances he can claim. This could arise during a period of unemployment or the first stages of self employment.

To transfer the married couple's allowance, make your application before the start of the tax year by completing Form 18 which is obtainable from your tax office. However, if you discover later that a transfer would have been justified you can apply retrospectively for a transfer for up to six years from the end of the year in question.

If you are living together you do not get the married couple's allowance but, if you have a child, be sure to claim the single parent's allowance.

If you have investments on which you are paying tax, transferring some of them to a partner who does not currently have sufficient income to use up his or her personal allowance and lower rate tax bands is also a way of saving tax. Savings of up to 40% on investment income are possible if one partner is a higher rate tax payer and the other a non-taxpayer. Such transfers of assets are often particularly relevant at retirement and can enable both spouses to make use of age allowance. (More about tax after retirement below.)

Normally any such transfer of savings has to be an outright gift, but you can opt to own investments jointly in equal or unequal shares and the income will be taxed accordingly, e.g. one half can be taxed while tax can be reclaimed on the other half. If you want to hold savings in unequal shares, you will need to apply for this by getting Form 17 from your tax office.

Even if both are paying the same rates of income tax, a transfer of investments could still be a good idea if you have made considerable capital gains which would make you liable to capital gains tax when the investments are sold. A transfer could reduce or remove this tax bill, since each spouse can claim an annual capital gains tax allowance.

If you are self employed:

You can reduce your taxable income by offsetting your business expenses and other allowances. You have to show that any expenses were incurred 'wholly and exclusively for the purposes of the business' for them to be tax deductible, though if you work from home you can deduct a proportion of your phone, insurance, fuel etc. bills. (For more on these points see Chapter 9.)

Topping up your personal pension plan is another way of getting tax relief. You can get extra tax relief if you top up on previous years contributions that were below the maximum. You can go back over up to six years. Use of the 'carry-back' provisions, which enable contributions paid one year to be treated as though they were made the previous year, can be particularly useful if you were paying a higher rate of tax that year.

If you are an employee:

Your employer may be able to help you save tax by providing you with some benefits which are free of tax and allowing you to choose how you take others in order to obtain the most tax efficient option.

Perks which are completely free of tax include:

Your employer's contributions to a pension scheme

Life and sick pay insurance

Work place nurseries

Cheap or interest free loans up to £5,000

Free or subsidised canteen meals for all employees

Luncheon vouchers up to 15p a day

Personal gifts, such as wedding and retirement gifts

Shares from a profit sharing or SAYE scheme.

Company cars are taxable if you earn more than £8,500 pa. The amount of tax you pay will depend on the value of the car and how much you drive it for business purposes. It could be more tax efficient to take a cash alternative instead if your employer allows you to choose. Each case is different, however, so you will need to work out how much tax you will pay on the car and compare this to how much tax you will pay for extra salary. If your employer pays for repairs, insurance and so on, which is not taxable, it may be better to stick with the car. (The taxable value of a company car is usually 35% of the manufacturer's list price, reduced by one third if you drive between 2,500 and 17,999 miles on business and by two thirds if you drive 18,000 or more. It will also be reduced if the car is four or more years old by the end of the year of assessment.)

Profit related pay is advantageous because it is tax free, providing it does not exceed 20% of your pay or £4,000 a year, if lower. Profit related pay can replace a proportion of your existing salary or be introduced instead of a pay increase. It can either be based on a stated percentage of the company's profits or be a fixed sum that varies in proportion with future profits. The disadvantage is that if your employer's profits go down so will that part of your pay.

Fortunately, there are a considerable number of tax efficient savings and investment schemes to choose from. Some are totally tax free, others have favourable tax treatment. But don't let the biggest and easiest tax savings be your only guide. High charges and poor performance can wipe out even the best tax concessions. High risk investments in particular should be treated with caution.

Here are the main schemes. More detail is given about each of them in Chapters Three and Four.

Tax free savings and investments:

National Savings Ordinary Account
The first £70 of interest is tax free.

National Savings Certificates
Both fixed rate and index linked certificates are tax free.

National Savings Premium Bonds
All prize winnings are tax free and there is no tax to pay when you cash in your bonds either.

TESSAs
A tax exempt special savings account enables you to earn tax free interest on your bank or building society savings.

Personal Equity Plans (PEPs)
You can invest in UK and EC ordinary shares, unit and investment trusts through a PEP and all your income and capital gains will be tax free. From April 1995, corporate bonds, convertibles and preference shares also qualify for inclusion in PEPs.

Tax Exempt Friendly Society Plans
These are regular premium ten year savings

plans with an element of life insurance thrown in.

Enterprise Investment Scheme

Any dividends or capital gains on shares of unquoted companies bought through this scheme will be tax free providing they are held for at least five years. There is the added advantage of 20% income tax relief and up to 40% capital gains tax relief.

Venture Capital Trusts

Any dividends or capital gains on investments in these trusts which will specialise in unquoted companies will be tax free.

Investors subscribing for new shares will qualify for 20% income tax relief and up to 40% capital gains tax relief.

Savings and investment schemes with some tax advantages:

Low Coupon and Index Linked Gilts

Any capital gains on these stock are tax free but interest is taxable.

Annuities

Part of the income from an annuity is regarded as return of capital and is tax free. The capital element varies with the age of the investor.

Life Insurance

Policyholders pay no tax on the proceeds from an endowment or other types of qualifying life insurance policies, providing they are held for ten years or three quarters of their term if less. However, the insurance company has paid tax on its funds so they cannot be regarded as totally tax free investments.

Investment bonds

As with endowments, the insurance company pays tax within these bonds so investors do not suffer a further liability to basic rate tax. One aspect which sometimes makes the bonds attractive to higher rate taxpayers or older investors is that withdrawals of up to 5% p.a. can be made without any immediate liability to extra tax.

When the bond is encashed, higher rate tax may also be avoided because of top slicing relief which means that the final gain (including any earlier withdrawals) is divided by the number of years the bond has been held, e.g. a £500 gain on a bond held for five years would be divided by five to give £100. This £100 'slice' is added to the investor's income and only if this portion is liable to higher rate tax will the extra tax be levied on the whole gain. Higher rate taxpayers may be able to avoid the extra charge altogether if they leave encashment until their income is lower or gift the bond to a spouse who pays less tax.

Special care needs to be taken if a bond is encashed when the investor is in receipt of age allowance since the whole of the gain will count as income for age allowance purposes and may result in loss of the allowance. (For ways to avoid this problem see **Tax and Retirement,** below.)

RECLAIMING TAX PAID ON INVESTMENT INCOME

On some investments, tax is deducted automatically from income at the basic rate before it is paid to investors. If you are a non-taxpayer, you can usually reclaim this tax. To do so you will need to ask your tax office for Form R40. If the amount of tax is more than £50 you can claim it immediately, if not you will have to wait until the end of the tax year.

However, if you receive interest on a bank or building society account you can get it paid without tax deducted if you complete Form R85, available from your bank or building society.

If you are a non-taxpayer you should generally avoid investments such as life assurance policies on which you cannot reclaim any tax which has been paid.

If you are a taxpayer but you have a low income which only takes you into the 20% tax bracket, remember that you can reclaim the difference if tax at the basic rate of 25% has been deducted from your investment income. This will apply to any building society or bank interest paid to you net of tax.

MAKING USE OF YOUR CAPITAL GAINS TAX ALLOWANCE

Many investors fail to make use of their annual capital gains tax allowance. If you sell assets, such as shares, for more than you paid for them and the difference falls within this allowance, you pay no tax on this gain. (You also get an indexation allowance to offset rises in value brought about by inflation - this allowance is equal to the rise in the Retail Price Index over the period you have held your assets, or since 1982 when it was first introduced.)

By selling investments with capital gains at regular intervals, you can in effect generate yourself a tax free 'income'. Some investments are more growth oriented than others. There are unit and investment trusts, for example, that specialise in growth shares. Zero dividend preference shares are useful because they are low risk and designed to produce steady growth over a fixed period.

If you fear your gains are going to exceed your

capital gains tax allowance in future years, you could take some gains in earlier years but still keep the same investments by carrying out a 'bed and breakfast' transaction - selling your investments one day and buying them back the next. This will naturally involve some expense but some stockbrokers, and unit and investment trust companies offer special deals to those who want to carry out such an exercise.

IMPORTANT: When comparing interest rates or investment yields, always make sure you are comparing like with like. Some rates are quoted 'gross' - before deduction of tax, others are quoted 'net' - after deduction of basic rate tax. Other rates may be tax free. A tax free investment may give you a better return even if the rate is lower than the gross rate on a taxable investment. For example, if the tax free investment is offering 6%, this is better than a taxable investment paying 7.5% because after basic rate tax you will be left with 5.625%, or even less if you are a higher rate taxpayer.

TAX AND RETIREMENT

Not paying too much tax is even more important when you reach retirement and are living on a limited income. Your state pension and any private pension you receive will be taxable so your main scope for saving tax will lie in how you organise your savings and investments.

If you are married, check that the ownership of your savings and investments is split between you and your spouse in the most tax efficient way. Husbands often qualify for a full state pension and have a private pension on top, while many wives reaching retirement still have very little pension of their own. Therefore it is often advantageous for a couple's savings to be put into the wife's name in order that her personal allowance can be utilised and the income from these savings be obtained free of tax or within the 20% tax band.

Remember to reclaim tax that is deducted from your investments at source on that part of your income that falls within your personal allowance. If you have income within the 20% tax band, reclaim the difference between that and the basic rate on any bank or building society interest paid net of tax.

Beware of entering the age allowance 'trap'. This is the point at which your income exceeds a given limit (£14,200 for 1994-95, £14,600 for 1995-96) and results in a reduction in your age allowance of £1 for every £2 of income over the limit until your allowance is reduced to the basic personal allowance. (This occurs at £15,710 for 1994-95, and at £16,810 for 1995-96.) Income which falls above this limit is effectively taxed at up to 37.5%. To avoid this trap choose investments which are tax free such as TESSAs or PEPs or produce capital growth. Withdrawals of 5% can also be made from investment bonds and these will not be counted as income for age allowance purposes. But when it comes to encashment the whole of your gain, including these 5% withdrawals will count as income. So you will need to ensure taxable income from other sources is reduced at this time or you may be able to give the bond to a spouse with a lower income.

TAX AND INHERITANCE

If your estate exceeds the Inheritance Tax limit and you don't want the Government to get a chunk of it when you die, you need to consider ways of reducing the bill as early as you can. During your life you can make some gifts free of tax. These include:

A basic annual exemption of £3,000 which you can carry forward to up to one year.

Small gifts of up to £250 a year can be made to any number of recipients.

Gifts to people getting married - up to £5,000 to a child, £2,500 to a grandchild and £1,000 to anyone else.

Gifts between husband and wife are free of tax on death. But if you leave everything to your spouse you may be missing a valuable opportunity to cut the total tax liability on your estate. Say you have an estate worth £250,000 - if you die leaving everything to your spouse who then leaves it to your children, tax will be payable when he or she dies. But if you leave £100,000 to your children when you die, and your spouse leaves them the remaining £150,000, there will be no tax to pay. But only do this if the surviving spouse will have enough left to live on.

On top of the various exemptions, you can make other gifts during your lifetime which may also be exempt from tax if you live for at least seven years after making them. If you die within this time, a reduced rate of tax may be payable. The scale is shown in the table below.

However, you won't save tax by giving away ownership of possessions and continuing to use them, because the taxman will treat them as though they have remained part of your estate when you die. So there is no point giving your home to your children and then continuing to live there rent free until the end of your life.
It is possible for one spouse to leave half of a property to children on death if you own your home as 'tenants-in-common'. But this may

cause problems if the children try to force the surviving spouse to move so that they can sell the house and cash in their share.

If you don't want to give your assets away during your lifetime, you could consider instead taking out a whole life insurance policy for your heirs (written in trust so that it does not form part of your estate on death) to provide them with the money to meet any tax on your death. The premiums on such a policy will be considered 'normal expenditure out of income' and will therefore be exempt from Inheritance Tax.

Rate of Inheritance Tax on Lifetime Gifts

Years between gift and death	Rate of tax
Up to 3 years	40%
3 - 4 years	32%
4 - 5 years	24%
5 - 6 years	16%
6 - 7 years	8%
More than 7 years	Nil

6 *The importance of pensions*

In the past, a pension was something that many people thought little about until they reached retirement. Younger people often expected they would have 'one foot in the grave' by the time they got to retirement so a pension wouldn't be needed for long anyway. Those who did think about the matter often took it for granted that the state pension would be adequate, and any extra pension from their employer a bonus.

Perceptions have changed dramatically. With people enjoying much better health in old age, retirement is now viewed as a time for living, doing all the things you didn't have time for while you were working. Indeed, for many people, retirement can't come soon enough. Retiring early to escape the rat race is becoming ever more popular. At the same time, however, people's assumptions about their pensions are changing. The Government has stated clearly that state pensions will go down in the future because it will not be able to foot the bill for the growing proportion of the population over pension age in the next century. People are now recognizing the paramount importance of building up their own private pensions through an employer's pension scheme or their own personal pension policy.

Fortunately, following the Maxwell pension scandal which rocked the confidence of many people in their employers' pension schemes, the Government has now tightened up the regulation of these schemes and proposed the establishment of a compensation fund in case anything goes wrong. The misselling of personal pension policies to those who would have been better off remaining in their employers' schemes has also been stopped. Now it is up to you to get the best out of the pension schemes available if you want an adequate pension. Remember it is never too early or too late to do something about it.

In case you need any further persuasion about the need to make pension planning a top priority, consider the following table of average life expectancies at different ages. It shows that a man retiring at age 60 has a life expectancy of 16 years. A woman in the same position can expect to live 21 years. Note that these are only average figures which means that though half the men aged 60 will not survive to age 80 the other half will survive even longer. If younger men knew that if they retire at 60 they have a one in three chance of being alive at age 85, they may start to look at pension planning in a rather different way.

LIFE EXPECTANCY

Age	Men	Women
	Years	Years
55	20	25
60	16	21
65	13	17
70	10	13
75	8	10
80	6	8
85	4	5

WHY A PENSION?

Using a pension plan to save for retirement has clear advantages over any other form of savings. Successive Governments have encouraged private pensions through tax incentives and look like continuing to do so in the foreseeable future.

These tax incentives are:

Contributions to a pensions scheme qualify for tax relief

Pension funds pay no UK taxes, so they can build up faster than taxed investments

Pension benefits can be taken in a tax efficient way, in part as a tax free lump sum.

WHAT MAKES UP YOUR PENSION?

The first step in pension planning is to get an idea of exactly what you can expect from your existing pension arrangements. Your pension can come from up to three sources - the state, your employer or your own personal pension plan.

THE STATE

There are two main types of state pension which are paid from state retirement age, which is 65 for men and, currently, 60 for women. In the future, women will also have to wait until age 65 for their pension, though this increase in age is being phased in over a ten year period between 2010 and 2020 (for more details see Chapter 11).

THE BASIC STATE PENSION

To qualify for a full basic state pension you must have paid (or been credited with) National Insurance Contributions for approximately 90%

of your working life. So, currently, a woman needs 39 years of contributions and a man 44 years. If you haven't contributed for this long, then you'll get a reduced pension but you must have a contribution record of at least a quarter of your working life to qualify for any pension at all. It could be worth making extra voluntary contributions if you have an insufficient record. The Department of Social Security can give you a forecast of your expected pension if you apply on Form BR19. (Available from DSS offices.)

Credited contributions are given to those who are out of work and are claiming unemployment benefit or income support, or who have home responsibilities and are claiming child benefit or attendance allowance. Men over the age of 60 who are no longer working automatically qualify for credits.

Married women who have paid the married woman's reduced NI contribution do not qualify for a pension in their own right. However, when a husband reaches age 65, he will receive an extra pension for his wife based on his own contributions.

The basic pension is upgraded each year in line with the increase in the Retail Price Index, but this means that it is falling steadily as a proportion of average earnings which tend to rise faster. For 1994/95 the single person's pension is £57.60, while a married couple gets £92.10. From April 1995 the rates are £58.85 and £94.10 respectively.

If you are self-employed, the basic old age pension is the only pension you will receive from the state.

STATE EARNINGS
RELATED PENSION
SCHEMES (SERPS)

If you are an employee, you may belong to SERPS which provides an additional state pension related to the level of your earnings on which you pay National Insurance contributions. If you retire before April 1999, you will get a pension of 25% of these earnings averaged over the period since 1978 when SERPS was introduced. If you retire after that date, the proportion will fall. Reductions to SERPS made by the Conservative government will be phased in after that until, from 2037 onwards, this pension will fall to only 20% of your lifetime's earnings. Like the basic state pension SERPS is index linked. A widow's pension is also provided. It is no longer compulsory to be a member of SERPS. If you are a member of your employer's pension scheme you may be automatically opted out. If not, you can decide for yourself. The pros and cons of opting out of SERPS are discussed later in this chapter.

YOUR EMPLOYER

If you are an employee, then you may belong to an occupational pension scheme. Membership of an employer's pension scheme can no longer be made compulsory but it usually makes good sense to join it. You will normally have to pay a contribution of around 5% of your salary. Your employer will top up your contributions. If you don't join the scheme, you will normally lose out on your employer's contribution towards your pension. Some schemes are 'non-contributory' so the employer foots the bill for the whole scheme.

The pension you receive from your employer will depend on the type of scheme offered and the length of time you have worked for that employer. The maximum pension you can receive is two thirds of your salary at retirement.

The best schemes are known as 'final salary schemes' because your pension at retirement will be calculated as a certain proportion of your final salary for each year that you have worked for the company. In most final salary schemes, you will get 1/60th of pay for each year of service (a less good scheme will give you 1/80th) but this means that you have to work 40 years with a company to get the maximum pension of two thirds of your final salary.

The other type of pension schemes are known as 'money purchase' schemes. These rely on all contributions (both from yourself and your employer) being invested in a fund which builds up through capital growth and reinvested income. These funds are usually managed by insurance companies. At retirement, your pension will depend not on your final salary (except for calculating the maximum amount permitted) but largely on the value of your pension fund. Consequently much depends on the skill of the investment managers. The level of interest rates at the time you retire will also be an important influence as they will determine the level of regular pension your fund will generate through the purchase of an annuity.

Money purchase schemes tend to be favoured by small employers, though some larger companies are now switching to these schemes also because of the mounting costs of providing final salary schemes. Both types of schemes must have the same retirement ages for men and women nowadays. Most employers have opted for 65 but with some schemes the normal retirement age is 62.

It is important, regardless of what scheme you belong to, to get as good an idea as you can of what your pension will be worth when you retire (and don't forget to base it on today's money so that you can relate it to your current salary). However, don't assume that the terms and conditions of your scheme will always be the same as they are today. It is best to ask your own pension department exactly what your pensionable service will be at retirement and what kind of income you can expect.

You should also check out how generous your employer is to retired employees. Certain pension increases are obligatory nowadays but your employer may provide extra discretionary increases.

A PERSONAL PENSION

If you are self-employed, or employed by a company which does not have a pension scheme, then you can take out a personal pension plan. If you have decided to opt out of SERPs (more detail on this below) you will also have your National Insurance contributions paid into a personal pension.

The more you save in a personal pension plan, the larger your pension should be on retirement. As a rough rule of thumb, every £10,000 you build up in a pension fund will produce a pension of around £1,000 p.a., so a fund of £100,000 would provide you with a pension of about £10,000. Don't be put off, if you feel you won't be able to save enough. Save as much as you can afford now and increase your contributions when you have more to spare.

Don't forget that you get tax relief on your pension savings. For this reason, there are limits on how much of your income you can save in a personal pension but they are generous and increase with age. Few people save the maximum. The percentage limits are shown in the table, though there is also a monetary limit if you are a high earner.

You can make either regular or lump sum savings. Charges tend to be lower on lump sum contributions but many people like the discipline of making regular savings. You are not limited to one pensions provider, so using a combination of both contribution methods is often a good way of spreading your contributions across different types of pension schemes with different providers.

Contribution limits to personal pension plans	
Age on 6 April	**% of net relevant earnings***
Up to 35	17.5
36-45	20.0
46-50	25.0
51-55	30.0
56-60	35.0
61-74	40.0

*Up to a maximum of £76,800 for 1994/5 and £78,600 for 1995/6

All companies now have to show in cash terms how much you pay in commission to sales staff and other costs and expenses associated with your pension policy. But cost considerations are only one aspect of choosing the right pension policy. Finding pension providers with good investment track records is vital. And it is equally important to ensure that the policy is flexible - that you can vary your contributions, stop and restart them again and retire early without being penalised. Ask about all these things before making your final choice.

CHOOSING A
PERSONAL PENSION

You have a wide choice of pension providers - insurance companies, banks, unit and investment trust companies. The policies on offer fall into two main types - with profits and investment linked.

With-profits policies

These are traditional contracts aiming to provide steady growth. Your contributions are invested in funds which contain a mixture of shares, property and fixed interest securities. The value of your policy increases at a declared growth rate or through bonuses, which reflect the profits made by the company. In order to give a smooth build up of returns, some profits are held back when investment conditions are good to cushion bonus falls when markets fall. At retirement a final bonus may be added to reflect rises in capital values over the term.

Investment linked

This type of policy has become more popular in recent years because of the investment choices offered and the more transparent structure. You can normally choose from a variety of investment funds investing in assets such as UK or overseas shares, property, fixed interest securities or cash, or managed funds which hold a mixture of these assets. Some unit and investment trust groups also offer pensions linked to their trusts.

Your contributions purchase investment units which can fall as well as rise in value in line with the market value of the underlying assets. The most popular investment choice is usually the managed fund, but policyholders are well advised to switch into a safer fund such as a fixed interest or cash fund shortly before retirement. Some companies offer to switch your funds automatically as you draw near retirement.

The suitability of the different types of policies will often depend on how long you have until retirement. The longer there is, the more risk you can afford to take. So if you have ten or more years to go, an investment linked contract can be used. If there is five years or less, a fixed interest or cash based contract may be safest. Alternatively some policyholders prefer to make modest savings into a with-profits contract as a basis, and to top up with single premiums in investment linked contracts.

Before taking out a pension plan, compare companies' past performance results by looking at surveys carried out in magazines such as *Money Management.*

If you took out a pension plan prior to 1st July 1988, you will have what is known as a 'Section 226' scheme or a 'Retirement Annuity Contract'. Anybody with such a plan can continue to contribute to it until they reach retirement.

OPTING OUT OF SERPS

You can choose to opt out of the State Earnings Related Pension Scheme. But you need to consider the matter carefully. If you decide to opt out, part of your National Insurance contributions will be paid into a personal pension plan of your choice. Whether this will provide a higher pension will largely depend on the level of contributions made and the performance of your personal pension plan.

The size of the National Insurance rebates will depend on how much you earn and your age. As a rough rule of thumb it is not advisable to opt out of SERPS if you are on low earnings, i.e. less than around £8,000 in 1995, because your contributions may be eaten up by charges. As regards age, you should only consider opting out if you are in your twenties or early thirties. After that, it may be a good idea to opt back into SERPS. However, the Government is planning to introduce age related rebates which could change these calculations. Ask your pension provider or a financial adviser for more information to help you make a decision.

The investment performance of your pension provider will have a crucial impact on the size of your pension if you opt out. Whether it is better than a SERPS pension will depend on the returns achieved compared to how much the Government of the day is paying out in state pensions.

OPTING OUT OF YOUR EMPLOYER'S PENSION SCHEME

You do not have to sign up for your employer's pension scheme nowadays. However, it is almost always best to do so for the simple reason that if you do not you lose out on your employer's contribution to your pension. If you take out your own personal pension plan, not only will you have to pay all of the premiums yourself but you will generally have to pay higher charges. Under an employer's scheme, your share of the administration costs will be lower or your employer may pay all the costs.

Moreover, you will often receive extra benefits alongside your pension, such as life assurance and sick pay insurance. These will also be more costly for you to replace on an individual basis.

CHANGING JOBS

You are more likely to consider transferring out of your employer's scheme if you change jobs or get made redundant. When you leave an employer, you have a number of options:

1. Leave your contributions invested with your old employer's pension scheme. If you do this your pension must be re-valued in line with inflation or by 5% per annum,

whichever is less. Benefits left in a money purchase scheme will continue to build up after you leave.

2. Alternatively, you may ask for a **transfer value** - a lump sum equivalent to your accumulated pension benefits - which you can invest in your new employer's pension scheme. But the pension benefits you get may be less than those you had before.

3. A transfer value could instead be switched into a personal pension policy where the benefits will depend on investment performance.

4. You could use your transfer value to purchase a 'buy-out' (or Section 32) bond from an insurance company. This will give you a set pension and you may get extra benefits depending on investment performance.

Before transferring out of an employer's scheme, check out carefully what you could lose. If your old employer has a good record for increasing the pensions of its retired employees in line with inflation or making additional discretionary increases, you could be better off leaving your money where it is. It also gives you certainty. If you transfer to a personal pension plan, there are no guarantees about the size of your future pension. However, much depends on your individual circumstances so it is best to get advice from your pension scheme manager or a financial adviser.

Note: If you have been a member of a pension scheme for less than two years, your employer can simply give you a cash refund of your contribution less 20% tax. However, many will give you a transfer value.

IMPROVING
YOUR PENSION

Whatever your situation there are various ways you may be able to improve your pension:

If you are an employee and have a state pension:

Take out a personal pension plan
Even if you have decided you will be better off staying in SERPS, the state alone will not give you a comfortable retirement income.

If you are an employee and have opted out of SERPS:

Make voluntary contributions to your personal pension plan
The pension generated from your National Insurance rebates may only give a pension marginally better than SERPS so you need to top them up.

If you are self-employed:

A personal pension is vital because you will only qualify for the basic state retirement pension
Make sure your contributions are adequate. You may not be able to afford to make maximum contributions, but be sure to increase your contributions as your income rises and when you have extra resources make a lump sum payment.

Remember that if you cannot pay maximum contributions you can make up the difference in future years. You can back-date your contributions for up to six years and still claim tax relief.

If you are a member of an employer's scheme:

Don't be complacent.
Even if you are a member of a good employer's pension scheme, you cannot afford to be complacent. Few employees get the maximum benefits under an employer's

scheme because they are rarely with the same employer long enough.

If you want to top up your pension, consider making additional voluntary contributions (AVCs). You can pay a total of up to 15% of your salary into your pension so you can make up the difference on top of your normal level of contributions by saving through an AVC scheme. One of the major attractions of AVCs is that you get tax relief at your highest rates of income tax on your contributions and they are invested in tax free funds.

You have the choice of taking out an AVC sponsored by your employer or arranging one independently, known as a Free Standing AVC (FSAVC). An employer's scheme may be more cost efficient, but you could get better investment performance from an FSAVC. You will need to compare the investment performance of different providers.

EARLY RETIREMENT

Many people would like to retire early but find they cannot afford to do so. So if you hope to retire early, it is essential to plan your escape well in advance by boosting your pension as much as possible. Because you will need enough to live on, the most important single factor determining the timing of your retirement will be the size of your pension. But the type of pension scheme and the circumstances of your retirement will also have an influence.

Retiring early under the state scheme

There is no provision for early retirement under the state pension scheme, unless you become an invalid. Indeed, there is a danger that you may not receive your full state pension if you stop working early and cease to pay National Insurance contributions. So consider making Class 3 Voluntary National Insurance contributions to ensure you have an adequate record of contributions.

Retiring early from an employer's scheme

The majority of schemes nowadays have a normal retirement age of 65. If you want to retire early, start making AVCs as early as you can to make up for the smaller pension you will get from your basic contributions. Find out whether the scheme will apply an early retirement discount factor. Typically, the reduction in pension is around 6% for every year that retirement precedes the normal pension age. However, if you want to retire early because of ill health or your employer is offering early retirement in order to reduce staffing, the discount factor may not be applied.

To make up for the lack of a state pension, employers may be able to arrange an extra boost to your pension until age 65 in return for a lower pension later.

Retiring early with a personal pension

You can start drawing a pension from these plans from the age of 50, but check whether your insurance company imposes an early retirement penalty if you take your benefits before a certain age or within a minimum term. To accumulate a decent pension by the age of 50, you will have needed to invest the maximum contributions beforehand.

AT RETIREMENT

Taking a lump sum:

Some pension schemes give you a lump sum automatically at retirement. Others let you have the choice of taking part of your pension as a lump sum. The advantage of the lump sum is that it is tax free, while your

THE IMPORTANCE OF PENSIONS   113

pension is taxed as income. So you may be able to improve your income by investing this money in something which provides a tax free income, such as a Personal Equity Plan. It also gives you greater flexibility. It may enable you to pay off debts, such as an outstanding mortgage.

Getting the best out of a personal pension:
When you get to retirement, you do not have to buy your regular pension - your annuity - from the same company with which you have made your pension savings. Different companies have different annuity rates and so it is important to shop around to find the company paying the best rate. You can give your pension a substantial boost by doing so.

There are different types of pension annuities. Some pay a fixed pension, others grow by a certain percentage each year. There are also inflation linked and investment linked annuities. If you are married you can choose a joint life annuity to ensure your spouse goes on receiving a pension if you die first. Seek advice from an independent financial adviser who can also help you find which company is paying the best annuity rates as they can change rapidly.

Interest rates determine the general level of annuity rates. So if interest rates happen to be low when you retire, you suffer a disadvantage if you have to buy an annuity straight away. However, in future it will be possible to defer the purchase of an annuity until age 75 if you wish to do so, regardless of whether you have taken a tax free lump sum. You will be able to withdraw amounts from your pension fund during the deferral period broadly equivalent to the annuity which your fund could have provided. This will give you the option of waiting until you buy a pension in the hope that interest rates will rise.

7 *Preserving your independence*

When you are fit and healthy and earning a living, it is easy to overlook the financial problems which can occur if you suffer an accident or serious illness and are no longer able to work. The early death of a parent with dependent children is likely to cause not only emotional trauma but major financial hardship to the family as well. You can no longer rely on the state to provide the safety net it once did, and while your employer may provide some financial help, it is not something to be taken for granted and it is often limited.

Life assurance and health insurance can provide protection against these financial disasters. Yet most British families are under-insured. They may have some life assurance but often not enough to meet the needs which arise when early death occurs. Take-up of policies that provide a replacement income in case of long term sickness is even lower.

Many people adopt an 'it won't happen to me' attitude without realising they are putting loved ones at risk. And even if you haven't got a

PRESERVING YOUR INDEPENDENCE   115

dependent family, you need to consider how well you would cope on your own if you suffered a serious illness.

Before considering the different types of life assurance available and how you can protect yourself against long term sickness, it is important to decide how much cover you really need.

HOW MUCH INSURANCE DO YOU NEED?

Various yardsticks for the right amount of life assurance are sometimes suggested. One rule of thumb is that you should insure yourself for a lump sum equivalent to ten times your annual income. But your requirements will clearly vary at different times of your life. A young couple without children will not need too much life assurance. But if they are relying on two incomes to make ends meet, they should make sure they have enough cover to pay off their debts, such as the mortgage, so that if one partner dies, the remaining partner does not have to struggle alone to meet the repayments.

For families with dependent children the need for cover is greatest. The best way of working out how much is needed is to simply sit down and calculate how much income each partner would need if they had to manage on their own. Fill in the life assurance calculator below. Your partner should fill in the amounts he or she would need if you died in the 'you' column and you should do the same for your partner.

Even if one of you is not currently working because there are young children to be cared for, you should consider the extra income you would need to pay somebody else to look after the children. Certain expenditure may no longer be necessary. If your mortgage is already covered by a life policy, for example, the outstanding loan will automatically be repaid and so monthly repayments will cease. In other areas, it may be necessary to spend more, for example if you have a company car your partner may need to find the money to replace it and pay the running costs.

When you have worked out the income that would be needed, and deducted any income you will receive, such as a widow's pension, you can then calculate how much life assurance cover you require.

To find out the lump sum required to provide the desired level of income, you will need to make certain assumptions about future interest rates. Such a calculation therefore cannot be absolutely precise, so try to allow as much leeway as you can afford in your reckoning. After all, no widow or widower is likely to complain if they are left too much. The other factor to take into account is that what may seem to be a realistic sum now, could be whittled down by inflation by the time it is paid out. To get round this problem, you could choose an insurance policy that is indexed to increase with inflation or gives you the option to increase your cover in the future.

As a guide to deciding on the level of cover you need the table on the next page shows the amounts you would have to invest to provide various levels of income at different interest rates.

When you have worked out the amount of cover you need, look back to your financial profile and compare it to your existing life assurance, not counting those policies covering outstanding

Table 1
CHOOSING YOUR LIFE COVER

Annual income required*	Lump sum needed if following interest rates available		
	5% £	7% £	10% £
£5,000	100,000	71,430	50,000
£10,000	200,000	147,860	100,000
£12,000	240,000	171,430	120,000
£15,000	300,000	214,290	150,000

* No allowance made for income tax or inflation

debts such as your mortgage. This will show whether there is any shortfall. Try to repeat this exercise each year to make sure your insurance cover remains in line with your requirements and has not been eroded by inflation.

If you are married or living together, you must then decide whether to take out two separate life assurance policies or a joint life policy. Joint life policies usually pay out on the first death. They are often somewhat cheaper, but cannot accommodate differing levels of cover and after the first partner dies, it means the survivor is left without life assurance.

YOUR LIFE ASSURANCE CALCULATOR

	You	Your Partner
Income your family would need on your death (excluding repayments of debts covered by existing assurance, e.g. mortgage)	_____	_____
Less pension	_____	_____
Income required from life assurance	_____	_____
Likely lump sum required to provide this income (use Table 1 as guide)	_____	_____
Less existing assurance cover (not including cover for outstanding debts, such as mortgage)	_____	_____
Assurance cover required	_____	_____

When your children leave home, the need for the protection type of life cover will normally diminish but you may still need life assurance for other reasons, for example, in connection with business, or to cover inheritance tax liabilities.

TYPES OF LIFE ASSURANCE

TERM ASSURANCE

If cost considerations are paramount, term assurance could be your best choice. This is a cheap form of life cover because it pays out only if you die within the insured period, say 5, 10 or 25 years. There is no investment element so you get nothing back if you survive the term. It can be used to provide a lump sum or you can get a family income benefit policy which pays out a regular income. Term assurance can be used to provide for the repayment of outstanding loans. For example, if you don't have an endowment mortgage, a term policy can be used to cover your mortgage in the event of your death. This is usually known as a mortgage protection policy.

A basic term assurance contract provides you with a fixed sum of life assurance cover for a fixed period. However, if you think your need for life assurance will continue it may be useful to take out a renewable or convertible term policy which enables you to take out a further policy or to switch to an endowment or whole life policy at a later date, without further evidence of health. This means you will not be left without any life cover at the end of the term if your health deteriorates.

If you are eligible for a personal pension contract, it may be cheaper to buy a special personal pension term assurance policy as you will then get tax relief on your premiums. If you

Table 2

TERM ASSURANCE

Typical monthly cost of £100,000 of cover

	Age	Length of Term				
		5yrs £pm	10yrs £pm	15yrs £pm	20yrs £pm	25yrs £pm
Male						
	25	8	10	12	13	14
	35	15	18	22	25	29
	45	24	33	43	50	58
	55	55	82	100	118	n/a
Female						
	25	6	6	7	8	9
	35	15	15	15	15	16
	45	16	20	25	28	33
	55	36	52	60	70	n/a

Source: Allied Dunbar (minimum premium £15)

are a member of a company pension scheme, you may also be able to boost your life cover through an employer's life assurance scheme, or with a Freestanding Additional Voluntary Contribution Plan (FSAVC).

The drawback of term assurance is that unless you renew or convert to another policy, your life cover runs out at the end of the insured period. And if you do take out another policy you will have to pay higher premium rates to take account of the fact that you are older.

The advantage of a whole life assurance policy is that it will give you permanent insurance cover regardless of changes in your state of health and at premiums which remain related to the age at which you started your policy. In the past traditional whole life policies were a rather expensive option but the introduction of unit-linked whole life policies has brought the cost down. These policies offer high levels of life cover at modest cost, plus the possibility of some cash if you cancel your policy. The cost of the insurance is kept down by assuming a certain growth in policy investments when premiums are calculated. Policies are usually reviewed after ten years and then at five year intervals in order to check that growth has been at the expected level. If it has been greater than expected, your life cover will be increased, if it has been lower you may be asked to top up your premiums.

Another advantage of unit-linked whole life plans is their flexibility. You can usually adjust your life cover under the policy within

WHOLE LIFE ASSURANCE

Table 3
UNIT LINKED FLEXIBLE WHOLE LIFE ASSURANCE

Minimum monthly cost of £100,000 cover

Age	Male £pm	Female £pm
25	15	15
35	19	16
45	40	23
55	102	72

*Premiums reviewed after 10 years
Source: Allied Dunbar

certain limits to suit your changing circumstances. For example, you can take the maximum life cover when your children are small, reduce it when they leave home and perhaps increase it again later to cover possible inheritance tax liabilities. Cover can also normally be increased in line with inflation.One point to bear in mind, however, is that although unit-linked whole life policies can build up a cash value, they should never be regarded as a savings contract. Your savings can be more productively invested elsewhere.

ENDOWMENT POLICIES

Endowment policies provide some life assurance protection but they are primarily designed for savings purposes in the context of which they are discussed in Chapter 3.

THE COST OF LIFE COVER

Apart from the type of insurance policy you choose, the amount you pay for life cover will also be influenced by a number of factors including: your age, your sex, medical history, your current state of health, whether you smoke, the amount of insurance you want and your occupation and hobbies. The younger you are the lower your premiums will be, while women (who have longer life expectancies than men) are normally charged the same premiums as men four years younger than themselves.

If you want a high level of life assurance, or have suffered illness in the past your doctor may be asked for a medical report or you may be asked to undergo a medical examination. Single men may also be required to have a blood test to ensure they are not HIV positive. But even if you are in poor health, you may still be able to get life cover at a somewhat higher premium.

Whichever form of life cover you opt for, it is a good idea to put it in trust for your partner and dependants under a suitable trust. The best trusts are ones which allow you the flexibility to meet changes in your personal circumstances, eg on divorce or on the birth of children. Writing a policy in trust will ensure that the benefits are paid out immediately after your death, otherwise there may be a delay until probate is granted. It also enables the death benefits to pass to your children without falling within your estate and being liable to inheritance tax. Most life offices will be able to provide you with the trust forms for use with their policies.

Life assurance is essential if you have dependants but only around 20% of men die before age 65 and only 15% of women. You are more likely to suffer a serious illness which prevents you from working. The financial consequences are just as serious.

One form of insurance that can help in these circumstances is critical illness cover. It pays out a lump sum if you are diagnosed as suffering from one of a number of serious medical conditions including cancer, heart attack or stroke, or require a major operation such as heart bypass surgery or major organ transplant. Many policies also pay out in the event of permanent total disability so you would also be covered if you were rendered unable to work by a tragic accident.

Such conditions can cause a considerable

change in your lifestyle and there could be many ways in which a lump sum would be useful, eg to make modifications to your home, seek further medical advice or pay off debts.

Cover can usually be purchased as part of a whole life or endowment policy, so that you combine protection against both death and critical illness, or if you have sufficient life assurance, there are also 'stand alone' policies which only pay out if you suffer one of the illnesses during the period of cover.

The snag with this type of policy is that it does not provide comprehensive cover against illness such as back pain or stress which can also be debilitating. For wider cover you will need an income protection policy.

Table 4
CRITICAL ILLNESS PROTECTION

Monthly cost of £50,000 of cover to age 60

Age	Male £pm	Female £pm
25	15	15
35	26	26
45	52	43
55	71	58

Source: Allied Dunbar

INCOME PROTECTION INSURANCE

It has always been a good idea to have income protection insurance in case you suffer long term sickness or disability, but with the Government now setting tougher medical criteria for claimants, reducing sickness benefits and making them taxable, the need has become even more pressing.

The risks of suffering long term sickness are higher than many people realise. Statistics show that men are five times more likely to suffer an accident or illness that stops them working for six months or more than they are to die before the age of 65. Advances in medical science mean that more people are surviving illnesses and accidents that would have previously resulted in death, but they are not necessarily in a fit state to return to their former jobs.

Some employers offer a sick pay insurance scheme. Find out exactly what your company offers. Employers do not have to provide you with any more than statutory sick pay, but they may operate an insured scheme. This may be given as a benefit or you may be invited to contribute to the cost. If you are, take up the offer, it will be cheaper than buying cover individually. If it is a benefit, you still need to find out for how long you will receive a replacement income and how much, as you may want to top it up.

The best way to protect yourself and your family from financial hardship in the event of ill health is by taking out income protection insurance. In insurance jargon this is often known as permanent health insurance (PHI) because once you take out a policy the insurers can't cancel it whatever your state of health may be.

Under a PHI policy you can decide the amount of income you want in the event of sickness, but there is normally a limit of 75% of your earned income less state benefits. (The insurers don't want you to be better off sick than at work.)

Although it is possible to choose a level income,

it makes more sense to opt for benefits that increase by a fixed percentage or in line with a suitable index both before and during payment to ensure they maintain their real value. Bear in mind that if you are subject to long term disablement you could be drawing benefits for many years.

Apart from the amount of benefit, other factors that will influence how much you must pay for PHI include - your age, your sex, your health, your occupation, and how quickly you want the benefits to start.

There are some disabilities that insurers will not pay out for, commonly injuries caused by war or civil commotion, self-inflicted injury or abuse of alcohol or drugs. For women, restrictions are normally placed on pregnancy related conditions - some insurers exclude them altogether, others will cover them if they continue for 13 or 26 weeks after the end of the pregnancy. Also excluded may be injuries that occur during certain types of sports.

Table 5
INCOME PROTECTION INSURANCE
Monthly cost of a replacement income of £10,000 p.a. to age 60, assuming low risk occupation, such as office job

	Income paid out after:			
Age	13 weeks		26 weeks	
	Male	Female	Male	Female
	£pm	£pm	£pm	£pm
25	15	15	15	15
35	17	33	15	19
45	26	56	18	36
55	31	62	22	42

Source: Allied Dunbar

Another point to watch is the company's definition of disability. Most will pay out if you cannot follow your own occupation, but some will only do so if you are unable to follow 'any occupation' which is much more restrictive.

PHI cover lasts until normal retirement age. Traditionally policies have been on a non-profit basis, so unless you fall ill you get nothing back. However, in recent years a growing number of unit-linked insurers have started offering policies where a cash value accrues if investment growth within the policy has been better than expectations. But this is mainly only of interest if you cash in early, as towards the end of the term larger deductions are made to cover the increased risk of ill health so the cash value decreases.

If you are able to buy PHI cover under a company scheme it will usually pay you to do so as premiums tend to be lower. But if you are buying a policy individually, don't let price be your only guideline. With this type of insurance it is particularly important to ensure that the terms and conditions suit your requirements, and that the company has a good record of meeting claims. It may be wise to seek the help of a financial adviser when taking out this type of cover.

HOSPITAL CASH PLANS/PERSONAL ACCIDENT AND SICKNESS POLICIES

These policies sometimes appear to offer similar cover to PHI but at much lower cost. However, there are some vital differences.

Hospital cash plans, as their name suggests, pay you a cash sum while you are in hospital and sometimes while you are convalescing. But before taking one of these plans bear in mind that the probability that you will go into hospital in any one year is relatively low. And even if you are admitted, the average stay in hospital is less than ten days.

Personal accident and sickness policies pay out cash sums if you are unable to work because of accident or sickness but the period of payment is normally restricted to two years. Thus, if you suffered long term disablement you would soon find yourself without any income.

PRIVATE MEDICAL
INSURANCE

BUPA type medical expenses insurance is becoming increasingly popular and there is now a variety of different policies on offer giving different types of cover. The most expensive are the comprehensive policies which will pay for all of the costs of immediate private treatment at a hospital of your choice. However, these policies are very expensive unless you can obtain the cover through your employer. Sometimes it is provided as a free job perk but even if you have to pay for it yourself it will be cheaper than buying the policy individually.

There are other low cost policies on offer with restricted cover. One of the most widely sold has been the 'six week' policy which steps in to pay for private treatment only if there is a wait of more than six weeks for NHS treatment, after the initial consultation with a specialist.

Another type places a limit on medical expenses of, say, £10,000. This will probably cover most types of treatment but there could be a danger with a major health problem that the money might run out before the treatment is complete. Another approach is to give a restricted choice of hospitals. Others keep premiums down by only covering the cost of in-patient treatment, or asking you to pay the first part of the cost of treatment up to a stated level. The over 60s receive tax relief on their premiums.

Before taking out a policy check exactly what treatment will be paid for. Most will not pay for the treatment of a previously existing condition, though some will do so if the problem does not recur within a stated period.

LONG TERM CARE INSURANCE

A growing problem for many families is providing care for elderly and infirm parents and relatives. Until recently most people assumed that the NHS or their local authority would step in and provide free long term care, once an elderly person or their families were unable to cope. But this is certainly not the case. Local authority residential care is very limited and any care that is provided is means tested. If a person's capital exceeds £8,000, the full cost of care will have to be met from his or her own resources. The value of an old person's home will be included in the calculation of their capital unless a spouse or other elderly relative or dependant is still living there.

To help mitigate the cost of paying for long term residential or nursing home care, some insurance companies now offer special long term care insurance. There are broadly two types. One enables you to insure in advance against future costs by paying regular or single premiums. They will pay out if you are unable to perform a number of 'activities of daily living' such as getting dressed or taking a bath without assistance. The other type are lump sum plans which give immediate payments towards the cost of nursing home fees when the need arises. Payments are guaranteed for as long as care is needed so there is no danger of capital running out.

8 *Your home*

Home ownership is not the easy option it used to be. Mortgage rates have proved very volatile, tax relief has dwindled away and the Government is restricting the help it gives towards mortgage payments if you fall on hard times. Houses are not the sure-fire investments they once were either. The early 1990s saw house prices slump and over a million people ended up with mortgages larger than the market value of their properties.

However, people still need homes to live in and in the long term buying your home is usually better than renting, so property purchase remains a central part of our financial lives. It is normally a continuing concern also. Most people move house more than once and increase their mortgages. Even if you don't move you may consider switching to a cheaper mortgage or repaying your mortgage if you have some capital.

When looking for the best mortgage deal, it is important to study all the cost elements carefully. The loan, the unemployment and sickness insurance and the repayment method all need to be considered.

There are a variety of different mortgages to choose from nowadays and lenders offer a range of discounts and incentives, such as cash rebates, free valuations and free unemployment insurance. Don't let these things distract you from thinking carefully about which type of loan is right for you. Also try to look beyond the initial discount period to make sure you will get a good deal in the future. Find out what the lender is charging existing borrowers and whether this is competitive with other lenders. These are the main types of loans:

Variable rate loans:

These are the standard type of mortgage. The interest rate on your loan moves up and down in line with general interest rates, although many lenders nowadays only change your mortgage payments once a year taking into account any rate changes that occur over the period.

You may be offered a substantial discount when you first take out a loan, especially if you are a first time buyer, so that you pay less in the first one or two years. Such discounts are attractive because you will have other expenses to meet when you first buy or move. But you will need to keep in mind the future increase in your payments when the discount period ceases.

Remember also that mortgage interest rates have come down substantially in recent years and that it was not so long ago - April 1990 - that the mortgage rate stood at 15.4%. Over the previous two years homeowners had seen their mortgage payments rise by over 50%. Although politicians are promising lower interest rates in the years ahead, they could rise again. If your mortgage payments are a major part of your budget you may be better off opting for a fixed rate loan initially.

Fixed rate loans:

Most lenders now offer a fixed rate option where your interest rate is pegged at the same level for a number of years and then reverts to the lender's normal variable rate. Unless the fixed term is short, say one to two years, you will normally have to pay a somewhat higher interest rate than the normal variable rate.

You can get fixed rate loans of five years and sometimes even ten or twenty-five years. The advantage of a longer term fix is that if you are working within a tight budget you can be sure that your repayments will remain stable. One snag is that you won't benefit if interest rates fall again and it can be expensive to switch out of a fixed rate loan. If interest rates rise, you will have to be prepared for the possibility that your repayments will jump when your mortgage reaches the end of its fixed rate term.

The benefits of a short term fix are limited unless it appears that interest rates are about to rise. You could get a better deal from a discounted variable rate loan.

Capped rate loans:

A few lenders offer these loans which are half way between a variable and a fixed rate loan. The upper rate on such a loan is fixed at outset so the cost of your mortgage cannot go higher. However, if interest rates go down, you will benefit. While these loans appear to offer the best of both worlds, they are generally more expensive to start with and the capped rate is only guaranteed for one to five years. They also tend to be offered by smaller lenders, so it is important to find out how their usual variable rates compare to the usual high street lenders so you know what your future costs will be.

Table 1, below, shows how mortgage rates have varied over the last decade:

Table 1
HOW MORTGAGE RATES HAVE VARIED OVER THE LAST TEN YEARS

Date	Mortgage Rate
1.1.86	12.75%
1.1.87	12.25%
1.1.88	10.30%
1.1.89	12.75%
1.1.90	14.50%
1.1.91	14.50%
1.1.92	11.50%
1.1.93	8.55%
1.1.94	7.64%
1.1.95	8.10%

There are also a variety of ways in which you can repay your mortgage:

THE REPAYMENT CHOICE

Repayment mortgage:
With this type of mortgage you repay your loan gradually over the term which is usually 25 years. Each monthly payment you make consists partly of interest and partly of a repayment of capital. The advantage is that you know you are steadily reducing the size of your loan. There is also considerable flexibility with this type of loan. If interest rates go up, you may have the option of extending the repayment period to, say 30 years, instead of having to pay higher monthly payments. And you can normally repay your loan at any time without penalty. You are not locked into a connected savings plan though it is advisable to take out life assurance to cover your loan. The cheapest

option is a mortgage protection policy - a type of term assurance that pays off your loan if you die.

Endowment mortgage:

When you take out an endowment mortgage, your monthly payments consist of the interest on your loan and the premiums on the endowment. To keep your costs down initially, you may be offered a low start endowment, where the premiums build up gradually over the first five years.

Your premiums are invested in a with-profits or unit-linked fund. The endowment is intended to grow so that the payout at the end of the term is sufficient to repay the mortgage, and you may even get a cash surplus. You also get built in life assurance so that if you die early the mortgage can be paid off in full. However, if you surrender an endowment early, you will not usually get value for money so they are only worth taking on if you are sure you can stay the course.

Even then, there is no guarantee that a policy will produce enough at the end of the term to repay the loan. Some insurers will inform you if they believe your endowment is not on target to repay your loan, and ask you to increase your premiums. If you are in doubt about your policy, it is worth checking the position with your insurer. In the past, endowments have produced some worthwhile results, but only if held full term.

Personal Equity Plan mortgages:

PEP mortgages have become a growing trend in recent years because they are tax free and tend to be low cost. Like an endowment, you pay interest only on the loan and make regular savings into a PEP. You will also need to take out a mortgage protection policy to pay off your loan if you die.

PEPs are very flexible. You are not locked into a fixed term and if your investments grow sufficiently you may be able to pay off your mortgage early. But there are no guarantees that the PEP will produce sufficient growth to pay off your loan. You will need to look carefully at the investment performance achieved by the PEP provider.

Personal Pension mortgages:

With this method, you take out a personal pension plan (or use an existing one) alongside your mortgage. You pay interest only on the loan during the term and use the tax free lump sum from the pension policy at retirement to pay off the mortgage loan. Although it is not as cheap as other methods, it does serve a double purpose in that you are saving both for the repayment of your mortgage and a regular pension on top. It can therefore be an attractive option for younger people who cannot afford two separate policies. However, the disadvantage is that you will sacrifice part of your pension benefits at retirement. Therefore, while it may be a good idea to start with this method, it is advisable to separate your pension and your mortgage as soon as you can afford to do so and substitute another mortgage repayment method later.

MORTGAGE PAYMENT INSURANCE

Mortgage payment insurance has become essential for new borrowers. In the past anyone who suffered long term sickness or unemployment received immediate help with mortgage interest payments from the state. But from October 1995, new borrowers will not be able to claim income support to cover interest payments for the first nine months of unemployment. Existing borrowers will get nothing for the first two months and then only

50% of mortgage interest for the next four months.

Mortgage payment protection policies typically cover mortgage and related endowment payments for up to 12 months. There can be wide discrepancies in the cost of these policies and the exclusions, so buyers will be well advised to shop around rather than automatically accept the cover offered by their mortgage lender.

Another useful precaution is to ask for a 'waiver of premium' to be built into any mortgage related term assurance, endowment or pension policies. For a small extra cost, this ensures that your premiums are covered if you suffer a long term illness.

COMPARING THE COSTS

Borrowers should avoid making their choices on cost grounds alone. Each method should be compared on its merits. It should not be forgotten, for example, that while the personal pension mortgage appears the most expensive it does provide not just for the repayment of the mortgage out of the tax free cash sum, but for a regular pension during your retirement as well.

In practice, many borrowers prefer to mix and match their mortgage repayment methods. Starting off with, say, a repayment or pension mortgage initially and then adding or switching to, say, a PEP mortgage when they take out their second mortgage.

Table 2, on the next page, sets out the typical costs of repaying a mortgage, but these will vary according to your age and premiums charged by different companies.

Table 2
THE COST OF REPAYING A MORTGAGE

Typical monthly repayments required for different types of mortgage plans at varying interest rates. Mortgage loan £50,000.

Type of mortgage	Mortgage rate		
Couple of 30/27	8%	10%	12%
25 yr repayment	350	409	471
25 yr endowment	367	441	514
PEP (plus term assurance)	346	420	493
Personal Pension	463	537	625
Couple 45/42			
20 yr repayment	384	439	498
20 yr endowment	418	492	565
PEP (plus term assurance)	396	470	543
Personal Pension	567	640	713

Source: Allied Dunbar (except PEP source Fidelity)
Notes: Endowment premiums based on growth rate of 9.25%, pension on 9% pa and PEP on 12% p.a. Pension premium net of basic rate tax. MIRAS relief on mortgage interest - 20%.

SWITCHING YOUR MORTGAGE

If you have had your mortgage for some years, you may find you can get a cheaper deal if you make a switch. Switching to a mortgage with a lower interest rate will save you £85 a year from April 1995 for every one per cent less you pay on each £10,000 borrowed up to £30,000 (the amount on which you get tax relief), and £100 on each £10,000 borrowed thereafter if you have an endowment mortgage, or some other interest-only mortgage. However, you will need to offset these savings against the costs involved in making a switch. Check whether your current mortgage has a redemption penalty - a typical penalty is three months' interest but it can be more on a fixed rate mortgage. Even if you stay with the same lender you may have to pay arrangement fees and administration fees if you switch mortgages. If you move to a new lender, this may involve valuation and legal fees, plus local authority search and land registry fees.

Other factors to take into account include possible loss of tax relief on loans taken out before April 1988 for home improvements, or on a joint mortgage exceeding £30,000 taken out before August 1988.

REPAYING A MORTGAGE EARLY

If you receive a capital sum as the result of a redundancy, retirement or an inheritance, you may wonder whether to use the money to pay off your mortgage. Or you may consider making higher monthly payments to reduce your loan.

The way to work out whether it is worthwhile to repay your mortgage is to compare the return you earn on your savings with the interest you pay on your loan. As long as generous tax relief was available on mortgage interest payments for home loans of up to £30,000, it was often possible to get a higher rate of interest on your savings than you were paying for your mortgage. So it made sense to continue with this part of the mortgage.

With mortgage interest relief down to only 15% from April 1995, you are likely to find that your mortgage will cost more than the interest you can earn on your savings so paying off your loan earlier may be to your advantage. But it may still be better to retain your capital in case you need it for other purposes. A mortgage is a very cheap form of borrowing so if you pay off your loan and then need to borrow money later from another source, you could end up worse off.

If your mortgage is over £30,000, the argument in favour of repaying is stronger but if this leaves you with no spare capital, it may still not be worth the loss of flexibility.

However if you do decide to repay with a lump sum, check the procedure with your lender. You will need to make sure there is no penalty for paying off your mortgage early, even if it is only a partial repayment, since this may make it less of a good idea. Ask about the minimum repayment - sometimes it is £500 or it may be £1,000 - and when it should be made as some lenders will only take repayments into account at the year end. Similarly if you want to pay higher monthly payments, your lender is unlikely to have any objections but you should discuss your intentions first with your lender to find out how these extra payments will reduce your mortgage.

Household insurance consists of two elements - insurance for the building and insurance for your home contents. Many mortgage lenders now offer combined packages but it is often cheaper to purchase each element separately. Don't assume that you are obliged to stick to the insurance policy offered by your mortgage lender. Even if you take it out to qualify for a mortgage discount initially, you can switch to another insurer later if you find a better deal.

INSURING YOUR HOME

If you want to switch your buildings insurance, your lender may charge you an administration fee of, say £25-£30, for the privilege. Don't be put off by this. You may be able to save this much or more on a cheaper policy.

It is well worth shopping around for buildings insurance. The main yardstick used by insurers to assess premiums nowadays is your postcode, but discrepancies can arise with one insurer putting you in a higher risk category than another. Other factors such as the age of your house may also be taken into account by some companies. If you have not made any claims in the last few years you may also qualify for a no-claims discount. Check out the telephone insurers whose rates can be particularly competitive if you have not made a claim recently. But if you do switch remember to keep details of your old policy for a few years in case a claim arises which overlaps the two insurers.

It is worth checking from time to time whether your cover is still correct. If you have improved or extended your home you may need to increase your sum assured. Remember that you are insuring the rebuilding cost of your home rather than the market value. To help you make your own calculations, the Association of British Insurers produces a free leaflet called *Building Insurance for Homeowners* which can be obtained by sending a stamped addressed envelope to the ABI, 51 Gresham Street, London EC2V 7HQ.

For contents insurance, many companies now offer bedroom based policies to save you having to calculate how much all your possessions are worth. This is convenient and avoids the danger of under-insurance which can lead to your claims being scaled down. On the other hand if you have only modest possessions you may be paying for more cover than you need with a bedroom-based policy. So it is still a good idea to work out roughly how much your contents are worth and if you have some particularly valuable possessions make sure they do not exceed individual item limits.

If you want to reduce the cost of your home contents cover, look out for the following discounts:

No claims discounts
If you haven't made a claim for the past three years you may qualify for a reduction in premium with some insurers.

Security discount

If you install high quality locks on windows and doors, burglar alarms and other security measures you will normally get a discount.

Age discounts

If you are retired and in some cases over 50 you will usually pay less.

Voluntary excess discounts

If you are prepared to pay more of each claim yourself, e.g. £100, you will often get a discount.

Most policies nowadays are on a 'new-for-old' basis, which means you are given the full cost of replacing a damaged item with a brand new one. However, if you find this type of policy is just too expensive, remember that you can get 'indemnity' policies which allow you to insure your possessions for the present value taking into account wear and tear. Don't forget if you are working from home to check whether your working equipment is covered by your insurance policy - some insurers now include this cover free up to a certain limit, say £4,000. If yours doesn't or you have more valuable equipment, you may need to take out a small business policy.

PROBLEMS WITH MEETING YOUR MORTGAGE PAYMENTS

If you find that you are facing difficulties meeting your mortgage payments due to sickness, loss of a job or because your partner has left, it is very important to contact your lender as soon as possible. The earlier you approach your lender the easier it is to find a solution. There are various ways in which the lender can help. Your payments could be reduced by extending the mortgage term. Your lender may even be prepared to suspend payments for a short period. Or they could give advice on moving to a smaller property. Your local Citizens Advice Bureau is also an invaluable source of help and assistance.

9 *Working for yourself*

Self-employment is becoming increasingly popular. Between 1980 and 1990, the number of self-employed people doubled to 3 million. One in eight of the workforce are now self-employed and it is expected that the numbers will continue to rise as technology makes it increasingly easier to work from home.

There are many attractions in becoming your own boss but it is not as easy an option as it sometimes appears. The self-employed on average work longer hours for less money than employees. It also means taking on more responsibilities. You have to manage your own tax affairs and you lose out on the extra benefits you may have enjoyed as an employee, such as membership of a pension scheme, life assurance, sick pay, private medical insurance scheme and other perks.

Nevertheless, you can benefit from your new tax status and the employee benefits you have lost can be replaced or improved upon when you make your own provision. At the same time, you can enjoy the greater flexibility and satisfaction that can come from working independently.

This chapter deals with some of the main financial considerations facing those who are self-employed, either working alone or in a partnership. Limited companies are not covered and, indeed, unless your profits are over £50,000, you will probably be better off remaining self-employed as you are likely to pay less tax and certainly have less red tape to deal with.

If you are planning to move from employment to self-employment, consider ways in which you can prepare the ground ahead before you leave your job. Building up a cash cushion is certainly advisable since you could face considerable initial expenses setting yourself up in business before you can start generating an income. That income could also take longer to arrive than you expect. If you are dealing with larger companies you may have to wait several weeks or even months for payment.

MAKING THE TRANSITION

To enable you to budget, it may be a good idea to switch to a fixed rate or capped mortgage for a few years. A review of your mortgage situation is advisable anyway because once you become self-employed making any changes could be more difficult. Lenders are naturally cautious about giving new loans or re-mortgages to the self-employed and will normally require three years' accounts as evidence that you have a stable income. So try and sort out any changes before you become self-employed.

If you are unemployed you may be hesitant to turn to self-employment for fear of losing all your benefits. However, if you have a family and your income is low to start with you may qualify for family credit. Another benefit which may be available to you is the Government's Enterprise Allowance which will pay you £40 a week for one year while you get your business off the ground. To qualify you must have been unemployed for at least 13 weeks and be intending to work full-time at your new business. Ask at your local Jobcentre for details.

BANKING

To help you keep tabs, open a separate bank account for your business finances. This will have the advantage of keeping your business transactions separate from your private ones. Your monthly bank statements will be a useful record and will enable you to cross-check your own accounts.

You could just open a second personal account if your activities are modest. But if your bank spots you are operating it for business purposes, you may be asked to open a special business account. Like personal accounts, there are a range of business accounts operated not just by the high street banks, but by some specialist banks and a few building societies too. Some pay interest on credit balances. Normally you will have to pay transaction charges for each cheque, etc, though some accounts allow a limited number of free transactions during each charging period. Don't forget you can offset bank charges against tax.

Consider your future needs when choosing an account. If you are likely to be maintaining a reasonably high cash balance, then an interest bearing account will be best for you. If your stream of income is likely to be erratic and you think you may need a business overdraft or loan, make sure these facilities are available.

BORROWING

High Street banks are still the main source of finance for small businesses. They often provide helpful literature on the subject and if you do want to borrow it is a good idea to look through this before you approach your bank manager because it will tell you the sort of information he will expect from you. If you want to cover yourself against fluctuations in your cash flow, the cheapest way to borrow for a short period is probably an overdraft since you will only have to pay interest for the periods you are actually overdrawn.

If you need a larger amount of cash over a longer period, you should ask for a business loan. The length of the loan will be a matter of agreement between you and the bank. Try to aim for as short a period as practicable. The interest rate on the loan may be fixed or variable. Besides protecting you from increases, a fixed rate is often preferable because it makes budgeting easier. To give you a bit of time to get your business going, your bank manager may let you have a 'capital repayment holiday' for the early months of the loan during which time you only have to pay interest.

Don't give up if you are turned down by your own bank, you may have more success at another bank. You could also ask your bank manager if he knows of other sources of finance which may be available. Your local Enterprise Agency may be able to help. You can get in touch with them through the nearest office of the Training and Enterprise Council.

There may be regional or industrial grant or loan schemes designed to support new businesses in certain areas to which you can also apply. If you want to do your own research, a good source of information on bank accounts, loans, grants and other business services - who offers them, terms and conditions - is *Business Moneyfacts* which is updated quarterly and should be available through your local library.

TAX

The three main taxes you will have to pay on your business income are National Insurance contributions, income tax and value added tax. But VAT is only payable if your turnover exceeds £45,000 during the tax year 1994/95, £46,000 for 1995/96.

One of your first steps therefore should be to tell the Inland Revenue and the Department of Social Security that you have become self-employed or set up in business. Each can supply you with some useful booklets giving you more information about what your rights and responsibilities are. If you think you may fall within the VAT net, ask your local Customs and Excise Office for the leaflet 'Should I be registered for VAT?' which will explain when and how you should register.

National Insurance

If you are self-employed, you will normally have to make two kinds of National Insurance contributions - Class 2 and Class 4. Class 2 are flat rate contributions (£5.65 per week for 1994/95, £5.75 for 1995/96). They can be paid by direct debit from your bank account to the DSS. (See Leaflet NI.255 Direct Debit - The Easy Way to Pay.) Class 4 contributions are a percentage of your income between certain limits - at present you pay 7.3% of your income falling between £6,490 and £22,360 for 1994/95 or £6,640 and £22,880 for 1995/96.

Income Tax

As a self-employed person you will receive a tax return each year. From 1997 you will be subject to the new system of self-assessment. So getting to grips with your tax return now will help prepare you for the new rules under which you will have to calculate your own tax liability. Books, such as David Williams'

Don't Pay Too Much Tax if You're Self-Employed, will help you through the maze.

Though the self-employed have the same personal allowances and pay the same rates of tax as everybody else (for more detail see Chapter 5), you do have the advantage of being able to offset your business expenses, such as stationery, postage, insurance premiums on business equipment and interest on business loans. So it is very important to keep a note of all your expenses, as well as evidence that they have actually been paid in case the taxman wants to check.

The Inland Revenue stipulates that in order to be allowable, expenses must have been incurred 'wholly and exclusively' for business. Nevertheless, in practice if you work form home or use your car partly for business reasons, you will normally be allowed to split the expenses. You could, for example, deduct a proportion of your heating, lighting and power costs and part of your telephone bill.

If you buy items of equipment in order to carry out your business, such as computers or fax machines, tools or a van, you can claim tax relief through capital allowances. You can deduct part of the cost each year, typically 25%, until the full cost is met.

If trading losses are made one year, they can also be set off against any other taxable income you may have that year or carried forward a year and set against the following year's profits.

Income tax will normally be payable on 1 January and 1 July each year - be sure you put enough aside to pay these bills. The Inland Revenue is getting much tougher with those who pay tax late. You will be charged interest.

VAT

As mentioned VAT is only payable if your turnover is above the annual limit. Bear in mind that it is turnover and not profit - you could be making a loss and still have to pay VAT.

You can register for VAT voluntarily if you want to. This could have advantages. It means you can claim back any VAT you pay out on new equipment when you first start up. You may also feel it would be good for your business image if people think that your turnover is above the limit.

But it means extra paperwork. You will have to add 17.5% to your bills and you will have to submit VAT returns quarterly, though smaller businesses can opt to make annual VAT returns instead. But if you do this, you will still have to make regular payments of VAT during the year towards your final bill.

DO YOU NEED AN ACCOUNTANT?

There is no obligation for you to have an accountant unless you have opted for limited company status. Indeed you will probably be able to manage quite easily without one if you are in business on your own and your profits are low.

If your profits are under £15,000 p.a., the Inland Revenue will normally accept a simple three line statement as follows:

Income from work (as your trade)	£10,000
Expenses	£ 1,000
Profit	£ 9,000

(Details of your expenses will not usually be required unless you have claimed an abnormally high figure for the type of work you are doing which makes the Inland Revenue suspicious.)

To help you work out how much tax to pay, the Consumers Association (publishers of *Which?* magazine) produces TAXcalc, an IBM compatible software program, mainly for use by self-employed people. You supply the necessary figures and the program works out the minimum tax you are liable to pay.

However, if you feel unsure it may be better to seek the help of an accountant initially and then follow the pattern that he or she sets. And you should certainly appoint an accountant if you are in a partnership.

When choosing accountants, a good starting point is personal recommendation but be sure to check their professional qualifications too. The two leading professional groups are Chartered and Certified Accountants. A smaller firm may be able to give you a more personal service than a large firm, but if you are going to be involved in, say, importing or exporting, try and find a firm which has expertise in that area.

How much will you have to pay your accountant? There are no fixed fees - most charge an hourly rate so it will depend on the amount of time that has to be spent on your tax affairs. A good idea is to ask for an estimate in advance. You can set off the fees against tax.

STATE BENEFITS

Class 2 National Insurance Contributions entitle you to a variety of state benefits. Many self-employed people do not realise they can claim such benefits as family credit or sickness benefit. While they are not worth a tremendous amount, you should certainly not forego claiming what you are entitled to. Here are the benefits you can claim:

Sickness/Incapacity Benefit:

If you are unable to work due to illness for more than three days you can claim benefit. You will need a sick note from your doctor which has a claim form on the back. These benefits cannot be backdated so be sure to claim promptly if you are ill.

Under the old system of ill-health benefits which runs until April 1995, sickness benefit is paid for the first six months of ill-health and invalidity benefit thereafter. Your GP decided whether you qualified on the basis of his medical opinion and the nature of your employment.

From 6 April 1995, a new incapacity benefit is to be introduced to replace sickness and invalidity benefits. For the self-employed there will be no difference during the first six months. But for the remainder of the first year, benefits will be lower than previously and there will be a tighter medical test. If you are not fit to do your own job, but well enough to do something else, then you may be refused benefit. After 12 months, incapacity benefit will increase, but it will still be taxable.

Maternity Allowance:

Women expecting babies will be paid this allowance for a period of up to 18 weeks starting before or just after the birth of a baby.

Widows' benefits:

Widows can receive a £1,000 Widows' Payment when their husband dies, Widowed Mother's Allowance if they have dependent children and a Widow's pension thereafter.

Low income/unemployment benefits:

If you have a low income, are working over 16 hours a week and have at least one child under 18 living with you, you may qualify for family credit in order to top up your income. As a self-employed person you won't qualify for unemployment benefit if you stop working, but you can claim income support.

Retirement pension:

The self-employed only qualify for the basic state retirement pension, not the earnings related addition (SERPS). This is payable at state retirement age, currently 65 for men and 60 for women, and not before. (Between 2010 and 2020 a new retirement age of 65 for women is being phased in - see Chapter 11 for details.) The full state pension is only payable to those who have made NI contributions for 90% of their working life between 16 and 60 or 65, i.e. men must have contributed for 44 years, and women, currently for 39. If you have gaps in your contribution record, it may be worth making voluntary NI contributions.

These state benefits are no more than an extremely basic safety net. With no benevolent employer to help you through periods of sickness or organise your pension or life cover for you, it is therefore essential that you make adequate provision yourself. Don't rely on the sale of your business or business assets to provide you with some money in your hour of need because there is no way that you can

LOOKING AFTER
YOURSELF

guarantee that a willing buyer will come along at the right time.

The first priority if you have a family is to check that you have sufficient life assurance to pay off your mortgage and provide your dependents with a replacement income should you die. Make sure that any existing or new life policies that you take out are written in trust for your dependents, otherwise the money will go into your estate and business creditors could have first claim on it.

If you need to top up your life cover, a tax efficient means of doing so is to take out a term assurance in conjunction with a personal pension policy. Like your pension contributions, the premiums on the term policy will qualify for tax relief providing they are no more than 5% of your earnings and are within your pension contribution limits. A personal pension is a must if you are self-employed. If your resources are limited, you may feel it would be better to wait. Don't - the earlier you can put money aside for retirement the more value it will accumulate in the longer run, even if it is only a modest amount. A regular premium contract will provide you with a savings discipline, but make sure it is a flexible contract which allows you to vary your premiums and stop and start them without penalty.

The next consideration is your health. To cover yourself against financial hardship during a period of ill-health, take out an income protection policy, or permanent health insurance as it is also called. This will provide you with a replacement income until you recover. But none of these policies pays out immediately, the minimum waiting period is four weeks. The longer the waiting period the lower the premium, so if you think you have enough savings to tide you over, a policy with a three month waiting period would be cheaper. To avoid long periods off work waiting for treatment, you should also consider a private medical insurance policy.

(For more details on different types of pension and insurance policies see Chapters 6 and 7.)

The amount of insurance cover you need for your business activities will vary according to their nature and scale. If you work at home with a limited amount of equipment, say a personal computer and a fax machine, they may be covered by your ordinary household contents insurance policy. But don't take this for granted. Check with your insurance company. They will tell you whether you need extra cover or not. Be on the safe side because unless you inform them that you are working at home, you could find that the whole of your contents cover becomes invalid because you have not revealed that you are working at home. If you have more significant amounts of valuable equipment and/ or your business means that more people visit your home, you will probably need to increase your level of insurance including your public liability cover. It is now possible to get specialist home office policies but if your business involves, say, owning a vehicle and travelling to clients to provide a service, you will probably need a small business policy. These are normally sold as a standard package to provide the cover most small businesses are likely to need. Contact an insurance broker to find out which company can give you the best deal.

LOOKING AFTER
YOUR BUSINESS

10 *Children*

H aving children involves a considerable amount of financial decision-making right from the start. Parents have to decide whether one partner should give up paid work and care for the children, or whether someone else should be employed to do the job. You could base this decision on a series of financial calculations - balancing how much you would lose in salary and pension benefits if you give up work against how much it would cost you to employ a nanny. But for most people this remains a very personal decision.

There are plenty of other choices to be made. Decisions about the type of education, for example, and how it is to be financed if you opt for private schooling. Even if you do not have to pay school fees, parents nowadays must consider the cost of maintaining their children as students if they enter further education.

A CHECKLIST FOR
SUCCESS

Then there are decisions to be made about children's savings, be they a few pounds a child receives for a birthday or Christmas, or serious money being set aside to provide a nest egg for children or grandchildren for the future.

And if you haven't made one already, you should not forget the need to make a will. There are good financial reasons for doing this at any time, but once you have children, a will also enables you to specify who should act as their guardians in the event of your early demise.

If you decide in advance that you are going to educate your children privately, then the sooner you start putting money aside for the school fees the better. At current fee levels, the total cost per child can be over £100,000. Any savings you can make beforehand will help to reduce the burden. All may not be lost if you have left it to the last minute, though, since there are loan schemes available.

PROVIDING FOR
SCHOOL FEES

When you are weighing up the costs of going privately, remember to take into account the likelihood of future increases in school fees. Although increases have slowed down in recent years, fees have tended to rise faster than the rate of inflation.

Another important factor to consider is how the fees would be paid if you died or suffered long term sickness. Don't forget to check that your life assurance is adequate and contact the Independent Schools Information Service for details of school fee payments protection schemes which provide funding for fees when a parent is disabled, made redundant, becomes involuntarily unemployed (i.e. if self-employed) or dies.
Table I on the next page gives a rough idea of the current cost of private schooling.

Table 1
APPROXIMATE RANGE OF SCHOOL FEES PER YEAR

	Prep schools	Girls' senior schools	Boys' senior schools
Boarding	£4,800-£8,700	£6,900-£10,800	£6,900-£11,400
Day Schools	£2,100-£6,000	£3,300-£6,600	£3,300-£8,400

* Source: Independent Schools Information Service

REGULAR SAVING FOR SCHOOL FEES

Although some companies offer special 'school fees plans', they are generally only life insurance saving products that have been packaged for the purpose. In fact, it is often advisable to use a combination of different savings schemes depending on how long it is until you need the money.

Since you can afford to take few risks with your savings, you will need to focus mainly on secure investments. For money needed within around three years, a building society account is the safest choice. A postal account often offers the best deal. If you have five years in hand, open a TESSA (tax exempt special savings account) with a bank or building society. Even if you cannot leave the money invested for the full five years necessary to qualify for tax free interest, the after tax returns are competitive. Index linked National Savings Certificates are another good choice. They are tax free and pay out a return equal to inflation, plus an interest rate bonus. Few other investments can give these guarantees.

For longer term savings, parents were traditionally advised to take out endowments.

But today many people are opting for Personal Equity Plans (PEPs) which are lower cost and more flexible than endowments as well as having the major attraction of being tax free. For fees starting in three to five years' time, you should save through a low risk fixed interest PEP. For periods of five years plus, a unit or investment trust equity income PEP is likely to provide better real returns.

According to the Independent Schools Information Service, funding school fees in advance out of a lump sum can reduce eventual costs by as much as a half or even two thirds. A combination of investments is usually the best approach. Building society and National Savings products provide security. If you invest the maximum lump sum in a TESSA each year or in a special 'feeder' account, some banks and building societies pay higher rates of interest .

**LUMP SUM INVESTMENT
FOR SCHOOL FEES**

Another low risk investment likely to provide somewhat higher returns than gilts or cash deposits is the zero dividend preference shares of investment trusts. These shares provide steady capital growth over a fixed period which is tax free if it falls within your annual capital gains tax exemption. A series of shares maturing in successive years could be used to fund regular school fees payments.

Personal equity plans (PEPs) are somewhat more risky but they can provide higher returns and they are tax free and cost efficient. Choose fixed interest PEPs for periods of three to five years and unit or investment trust general equity PEPs for longer periods. You can put lump sums of up to £6,000 p.a. into a general PEP. A husband and wife together could put in £12,000.

Educational trusts:

If interest rates are high, it may be worth considering an educational trust scheme. These are annuity based schemes which are set up to start paying termly fees at a future date for a fixed period. This method can be advantageous for higher rate taxpayers because the trusts' charitable status enables them to make tax free payments direct to the school of your choice.

Educational trusts can bring savings even when fees are due to start immediately. Most annuities are written on a non-profit basis, and payments can be either fixed or set to escalate at an agreed percentage each year. This sort of trust can be good value if annuity rates are high and fees are due to start within five years. However, if there are still three to five years to go a unit-linked or with-profits annuity could produce better returns because payments will reflect investment growth.

A further tax benefit of an educational trust for a parent or guardian is that the money invested will fall outside their estate for inheritance tax purposes even if they die within seven years. This can also apply to money invested by other adults, but only if they waive their right to cash in their plan.

School composition fees:
Another way of using a lump sum is to pay fees to the school in advance. These schemes allow for some discount on the termly fees. If a lump sum payment is made at the time of the pupil's entry to cover all or part of the likely fees, you might get a reduction of some 15% of the fees covered. However, a lump sum put down four years in advance could reduce fees by as much as 50%. For details, parents will need to contact the bursar of the

school concerned for particulars. Remember to ask what the position is if the child needs to be transferred to another school.

BORROWING TO
FINANCE SCHOOL FEES

Many parents fail to plan in advance for school fees and find themselves struggling to meet all the costs out of income. If you are in this position you may need to borrow money, though check first whether grandparents may be prepared to help, if they have not done so already.

If you need to borrow, the best solution is usually to take out an additional mortgage on the family home, assuming it is worth more than your current mortgage. Various schemes are available which typically allow parents to borrow between 75% and 85% of their property value less any outstanding mortgage. Once the facility is arranged, the loan can usually be drawn down as it is needed to pay fees. Interest is only charged on the money that has actually been borrowed. However, the interest rate may be slightly higher than for a standard mortgage scheme. The capital will be repayable at the end of a set period of 10 to 25 years and the lender will normally require you to take out an endowment or a PEP to cover repayment.

PAYING FOR A
UNIVERSITY EDUCATION

Most students' college fees are still paid by the state. However, the grant which students get towards their living expenses is being steadily reduced and replaced by student loans, repayable when the student starts paid employment. Evidence suggests that many students are also taking on extra debt in order to make ends meet.
Even the basic grant is not provided to all.

Parents of students are means tested to assess what they can afford and the majority end up having to contribute at least part of their children's maintenance grant. These can end up being hefty sums, especially if you have several children. It is estimated that by the year 2004, assuming inflation of 4.5% a year, the cost of supporting a student through a three year university course will be over £21,000.

Saving in advance obviously makes a great deal of sense and most of the saving and investment ideas mentioned above for school fees planning would be equally useful for this purpose. It is also worth making use of your children's tax position as explained below.

CHILDREN'S SAVINGS

There are a variety of considerations to be taken into account when deciding on the right investment for children. Tax is one of them. Children do not qualify for tax free TESSAs or PEPs, but they can normally receive investment returns free of tax if you give your choices some thought beforehand. Bear in mind the different tax treatment of money given by parents as opposed to cash gifts from other relations or friends. For this reason, it may sometimes be wise to keep gifts separate.

Money from parents:
Any income or interest generated by this money is only tax free as long as it does not exceed £100. If the income is more than £100 a year, then the whole amount (not just the excess) is taxed as though it is the parent's income. However, this rule applies to money given by each parent, so a child can enjoy a tax-free £200 if both parents make gifts.

Money from others:

Any income or interest generated by this money will be tax free as long as it does not exceed the child's tax allowance. Children have the same personal tax allowance as adults so make sure that if any tax is deducted at source then it is reclaimed on the child's behalf (ask your tax office for form R40). They also have their own capital gains tax allowance.

The next step is deciding on the nature of the savings - should they be accessible so the child can dip into them when money is needed or are they designed for the longer term to provide a nest egg for when they become adults or as a contribution towards funding their education?

Fun money:
The best place for childrens' own savings and one which can help them learn more about managing their own money is an instant access bank or building society account. Here they can deposit and withdraw their own money (once they can provide a signature) and save up for holidays, toys or presents. Most banks and building societies have special accounts for children which are designed to make saving fun and attractive. Freebies such as money-off vouchers, money boxes, magazines and wall charts are provided. You can also help the child learn about interest and compare the rates offered on different accounts.

So that interest is paid into the child's account free of tax, a parent or guardian will need to complete form R85, which the bank or building society will supply.

Serious money:

When you are building a nest egg for a child's future, you should apply the same rules as you would with your own savings, starting off with safety first low risk investments, such as National Savings, before moving on to medium and higher-risk investments.

National Savings has a special Children's Bonus Bond which is ideally suited for gifts from parents because the returns are tax free and will not count towards the £100 tax free limit on income to their gifts which otherwise applies. The bond offers a fixed return over a five year term and can be bought for children under 16. Once the bond has been held for five years, it can either be cashed in or held at the prevailing rate until the holder reaches the age of 21. The minimum investment is £25 and the maximum is £1,000 per child.

Money from other sources can be used to buy National Savings Capital Bonds, which also pay a fixed rate over five years. Although the interest is taxable, there will be no tax to pay as long as it falls within the child's personal allowance. The minimum investment is £100 and the maximum is £250,000.

Unit or investment trust saving or investment schemes are good for longer term investments for children. Although they cannot normally be held in the child's own name until he or she reaches the age of 18, they can be held in the parent's name and designated with the child's name and then transferred when the child comes of age. Any income generated on these investments will be taxed at source but this tax can be reclaimed on the child's behalf providing it falls within the £100 limit if it is money from the parents, or within the child's tax allowance if it is a gift from another source.

Parents can reduce tax deductions by investing in trusts that aim to produce mainly capital growth. An offshore investment fund could also be considered as the money can be left to roll up free of tax until the child is over 18. When the child takes over the investment at 18, any capital gains or income can be offset against the child's own tax allowance.

If you are a higher rate taxpayer and you want to put larger sums of money aside for your children, and you don't want them to gain control of the capital too early, you could consider setting up an accumulation and maintenance trust. By doing so, you can avoid paying higher rate tax yourself on any income arising from your gift. However, there are strict rules about use of the income. As long as the child is under 18 it can only be used for the child's education or living expenses. Any remaining income must be accumulated for each child until at least the age of 18.

PUTTING MONEY IN TRUST FOR CHILDREN

Income within the trust will be subject to basic rate tax and an additional rate of tax making a total rate of 35% at present. For this reason it is often a good idea to invest the money in an endowment or investment bond where any income will be taxed at more favourable rates within the insurance policy itself or in an offshore investment bond where it can roll up tax free.

Normally such trusts come to an end when children are between the ages of 18 and 25 and the accumulated value is shared out between them. This money will be treated as capital in the hands of the child and no higher rate tax will be payable on the accumulated income. However, if you do not want your children to have the capital, then you can give them a right to the income only instead. The trustees can decide if and when the capital can be distributed.

INSURANCE FOR CHILDREN

Many parents overlook the possibility of insuring their children against injury. They often assume that if a child is injured during school activities, the school or education authority will have to pay compensation, but such a claim will only succeed if negligence can be proved. Moreover, many accidents happen outside school, at a sports club or in the home.

It is therefore a good idea to take out personal accident insurance for your child. These policies pay out according to a scale depending on the seriousness of the injury, ranging from loss of a finger or toe to total paralysis. While money cannot restore health, it can make things easier for the child or be invested for his or her future.

WILLS

Your children may automatically inherit part of your estate when you die, whether you make a will or not. But it may not be divided up in the way you intended. More inheritance tax may also be payable. Through a will you can make your wishes clear and possibly avoid family upsets. A will is especially advisable if you are living with your partner (and have not married), or you have remarried and have children from a previous marriage.

But first a word about the ownership of your home. What happens to your share of your home if you are married or live with a partner will depend on whether you own the property as 'joint tenants' or 'tenants in common'. Most co-owners are joint tenants. This means that when you die your share of the home passes automatically to your partner, regardless of a will or the laws of intestacy. If you want something different to happen you will have to change the form of ownership to 'tenants in common'. Your share of the property then forms part of your estate. This way you can leave your share of the property to your children. This may be particularly relevant if you have children from a previous marriage who you want to inherit your share. But a will is necessary to ensure that this wish is fulfilled.

If you don't make a will, your assets will be divided up under the laws of intestacy. Below is a simple guide to the rules though in practice they can be quite complex. (These are the laws which apply in England and Wales. In Northern Ireland and Scotland different rules apply.)

If you are unmarried and have no children: Your money will pass in the first instance to your parents or, if they are dead, to your brothers and sisters or their children, or to other relatives. (So if you are living with a partner who you want to inherit your money, a will is essential.)

If you have children but no legal spouse: Your money is divided among your children equally. (Here again an unmarried partner will lose out.)

If you are married but have no children:

Your spouse gets everything up to £200,000 plus your personal effects, plus half the remainder. The other half passes to your parents, or other relations.

If you are married with children:

Your spouse gets the first £125,000, plus your personal effects, plus the income from half the remainder. The other half goes to your children. On your spouse's death, his or her half of the remainder also passes to the children. (Stepchildren are not covered by these rules.)

Even if you are happy with these rules, there can be tax advantages in making a will. It enables each spouse, for example, to pass on assets free of inheritance tax, so that the 'nil rate' band can be used twice over.

It also means you can pass some money direct to grandchildren or great grandchildren. This can be useful if your children have already acquired assets and your money would simply push them further into the inheritance tax bracket. If they have to pass it to their children any income or interest arising from it will be taxed as the parents if the grandchildren are still minors. Whereas if you give the money direct to your grandchildren, your children will have fewer inheritance tax problems and any income generated will be set off against the child's own tax allowance. (For more detail on ways of minimising inheritance tax, see Chapter 5.)

If your wishes are simple, you could make a do-it-yourself will. But to avoid misinterpretations and other potential problems arising after your death, it may be safer to employ a solicitor. If you want to do something unusual like disinheriting a family member, if you have a business or you have assets overseas such as a holiday home, seeking professional advice is essential. If you don't already have a solicitor, enquire at your local library for a list of those in your area and then ring round and ask about the likely cost involved.

When you draw up a will you will have to name executors to carry out your wishes. If it is straightforward, using friends and relations may be adequate, but for more complex wills consider using the services of your bank, solicitor or accountant. This will be more expensive but it may be worth paying for their expertise.

Once you have made a will remember to review it regularly. If you need to make changes, don't just amend the original. You will need to add an extra part, a codicil, or draw up a fresh will. Make sure you keep your will in a safe place and inform your relatives where it can be found.

Even if you make a will, claims can still be made against your estate by anyone who you were wholly or partly maintaining prior to your death under the provisions of the Inheritance (Provision for Family and Dependants) Act 1975.

11 *Women and money*

There are two schools of thought about women and money. Some people argue that women have the same financial needs as men. Others believe that women's requirements are quite different. There are elements of truth in both these arguments. Clearly women face many of the same financial problems as men. However, there are significant differences in the way women's lives develop which must be considered when financial plans are being made, otherwise women can lose out.

At the beginning of their working lives there are few obvious differences. Young women usually enjoy a period of financial independence and relative affluence as they establish their career, though on average women working full time still earn 12% less than men. But as time goes on the pattern of a woman's working life tends to diverge from that of a man's.

If she has children, she will often spend a period out of paid employment and a further period working part time. Even if she returns to full time work immediately she is likely to find getting promotion more difficult because of employer attitudes. This will diminish her earnings and pension prospects considerably. A recent study by London University showed that by the age of 35, a woman who has had children is earning, on average, one third less than a woman who has not. On divorce women normally retain the main responsibility for the care of the children.

Another obvious difference between the sexes is that women live longer than men. Even after pension ages are equalised at 65, this means they will spend a larger part of their lives in retirement. Unfortunately, though, due to their lower pay and interruptions to their working lives they usually have lower pensions than men. Many women end up on the poverty line at retirement, dependent on income support. However, they may inherit assets from their husband which they can use to provide an extra income.

Because of their longevity, women are also more likely to need residential care when they become elderly.

Table 1
HOW LONG DO WOMEN LIVE?

Future life expectation at various ages

Current Age	Life expectancy (Years still to live)
20	58
30	48
40	39
50	29
60	21
70	13

WHAT WOMEN NEED TO DO

Women who want to take more control of their financial situation face an up-hill struggle. But here are some golden rules to bear in mind:

1. It is never too late to start your financial planning but the sooner you do so the better. For most women the time when they have the most disposable income is in the early years of their career before they have children so this is the time to save as much as you can.

2. Put pensions at the top of your agenda. We are all living longer and it is vital to ensure that you can enjoy your retirement free from money worries. Start contributing to your pension as early as possible.

3. Keep your planning flexible. If your circumstances change, you will need to have savings or pension schemes that do not penalise you if you lower or cease your contributions.

4. Don't rely on your partner. At least one in three marriages end in divorce. Make sure your interests are protected in any joint financial arrangements and don't necessarily expect to share his pension.

5. Review your financial situation regularly. Because your life and career is unlikely to follow a straight course, you will need to check what changes are needed to keep your finances on course to achieve your objectives.

THE IMPORTANCE OF PENSIONS

Recent statistics show how badly women fare in retirement. The Women's National Commission found that only 15% are on a full state pension. Half of female retired households in the UK survive on an income of only £50 a week. There is a desperate need for women to maximise what state benefits they are entitled to, take advantage of what employers can offer and wherever possible make their own savings in order to boost their pension prospects. Yet only around 2.1m women have personal pension plans, a further 35% of women employees are members of employers' pension schemes but this still leaves over 4m working women with no private pension provision at all.

The most important pension benefit for many women for some time to come will be the state pension. Women currently receive a state pension from age 60, assuming their National Insurance contribution record is adequate. In future, however, the state pension age is to be equalised for men and women at 65. There will be a phasing-in period between 2010 and 2020. During this time the age at which women qualify for a state pension will gradually rise to 65. Thus, women born before 6 April 1950 will still be able to draw a pension at age 60 while those born after 6 May 1955 will have to wait until age 65. Women born between the two dates can expect to retire between 60 and 65.

Some relevant dates and ages are shown in the table on the next page:

STATE PENSIONS
FOR WOMEN

172 MAKING THE MOST OF YOUR MONEY

Table 2
EXAMPLES OF NEW PENSION AGES DURING THE PHASING-IN PERIOD OF THE NEW STATE PENSION AGE FOR WOMEN

Date of birth	Pension Age	Pension Year
April 1950	60yr 1mth	2010
Oct 1950	60yr 7mth	2011
April 1951	61yr 1mth	2012
Oct 1951	61yr 7mth	2013
April 1952	62yr 1mth	2014
Oct 1952	62yr 7mth	2015
April 1953	63yr 1mth	2016
Oct 1953	63yr 7mth	2017
April 1954	64yr 1mth	2018
Oct 1954	64yr 7mth	2019
April 1955	65yr 0mth	2020

From: Equality in State Pension Age, DSS White Paper

The state pension comes in two parts:

1. The basic state pension

To qualify for the full basic state pension currently, you must have made National Insurance contributions or been credited with them for 90% of your working life, i.e. 39 years out of the 44 between the ages of 16 and 60 if you retire before 2010. If your contribution record is not sufficient you will receive a lower pension.

So beware - gaps can occur in your record if you spend periods not working or your earnings are below the contribution limit, £57 a week for 1994-95 or £59 for 1995-96 (this level is revised each year). You do receive NI credits, however, if you sign on as unemployed or home responsibility protection (HRP). To qualify for HRP you must be claiming child benefit for a child under 16 or be looking after someone who is receiving attendance allowance, or be getting income support so that you can stay off work to look after an elderly or sick person at home. For full details see DSS leaflet NP27 *'Looking after someone at home? How to protect your pension.'*

If you are not receiving credits you could consider paying voluntary National Insurance Contributions towards your state pension.

One of the advantages of a state pension is that it is increased each year in line with inflation. But it is such a modest amount, it can be regarded as no more than a very basic safety net. Yet if you are self-employed this is all you will get from the state.

2. SERPS

If you are an employee you may qualify for a further pension from the state under what is known as SERPS (the State Earnings Related Pensions Scheme). This scheme is designed to give you some extra pension linked to the size of your earnings. But since its introduction in 1978 it has been changed and watered down.

Since 1988, membership of SERPS has not been compulsory. So you may have decided to opt out, or be considering doing so, in order to have that part of your NI contributions paid into your own personal pension plan instead. The attractions of opting out are that you could obtain a higher pension and you have more control over your money and when and how your pension should be taken.

Women under 35 might benefit from opting out initially but only if they are earning at least £8,000-£10,000 per annum and expect to be able to contribute to a personal pension plan for two years or more. Otherwise, there is a danger that the contributions will be too small and charges levied on the pension plan will eat into its value and leave you worse off.

Anyone who opted out of SERPS in the past should review their decision regularly. The Government is expected to introduce age-related NI rebates soon which may make it more attractive for older women to remain opted out. But if your circumstances have changed, say, your earnings have fallen, opting back into SERPS may be a better idea. Each situation will be different, however, so it is worth checking your position with a financial adviser.

If you have not yet opted out, consider the matter carefully. For more detailed advice discuss your position with a financial adviser. If you are a borderline case, it is probably safer to stay inside SERPS. This will provide you with a guaranteed fixed percentage of your average earnings, while the pension you can buy with a private plan will depend partly on the investment results achieved by your personal pension provider and partly on the general level of interest rates when you reach retirement.

PERSONAL PENSIONS

However, a state pension will never provide you with anything more than a subsistence standard of living. All working women who do not belong to an employer's pension scheme should take out a personal pension plan as soon as possible. Even if you have opted out of SERPS you should top up your pension with extra savings.

The need for women to start a pension as early

as possible cannot be emphasised strongly enough. Ideally you should aim to save around 15% of your earnings every year throughout your working life and if you have not done in the past you will need to save more now.

The later you leave it the more you will need to save in order to achieve the same objective, as Table 3 illustrates. It shows that a woman of 20 who is prepared to save £55 per month now could expect a pension of £15,000 p.a. at age 60, whereas if she was now 40 she would have to save a hefty £310 pm to achieve the same pension.

Table 3
HOW MUCH A PENSION COSTS AT DIFFERENT AGES

Current Age	Typical monthly contribution required to provide pension of £15,000 p.a. at age 60 (assuming 9% p.a. growth rate).
20	£55
30	£126
40	£310

It is also important to bear in mind that such calculations assume the woman continues saving until retirement. If the 20-year-old took a career break to look after young children between the ages of 25 and 30, for example, she would need to increase her contribution to achieve her original objective, though this would still be less than if she had not started her pension plan until age 30.

Naturally such examples are purely hypothetical. Unfortunately, very few women do start their pensions so early or save consistently due to fluctuating earnings. The best advice is to start saving as much as you can, whenever you can. The contributions limits, tax advantages and different types of personal pension plans have been discussed in Chapter 6. A further very important question for women to ask before they take out a plan is how flexible it is - make sure the plan permits you to stop or decrease your contributions without penalty, should you take a career break or take a reduction in earnings. Both men and women can take personal pension benefits from age 50 onwards (though most people will not have saved enough by this age to make it a feasible proposition.)

A PENSION WITH YOUR JOB

If your employer offers you a pension with your job - take it. Though employers' schemes do not always meet women's needs particularly well, they do offer a number of advantages. One of the most important is that your employer will contribute to the scheme on your behalf, even when you take maternity leave. A range of other benefits may also be provided as part of the scheme, such as a widower's pension and life assurance. More details of company pension schemes can be found in Chapter 6.

In the past, most employers normally allowed women to retire before men but most have now equalised the pension age for men and women at age 65, though women may still be allowed to retire at the previous pension age without penalty.

WHAT HAPPENS TO YOUR PENSION IF YOU TAKE A CAREER BREAK

If you stop work for some years while your children are young, you will receive NI credits towards your state pension, but that is all. In an employer's pension scheme you will be protected during your maternity leave but not if you stay away for longer. And you cannot contribute to a personal pension plan during this time because you do not have any earnings. But if your partner wants to cut the family's tax bill during this period, it may be a good idea for him to transfer some of his savings to you in order to take advantage of your independent tax status, as explained in Chapter 5. By investing this money in something long term like a Personal Equity Plan, you will be able to accumulate a lump sum for your retirement.

When you return to work, there may be opportunities for you to top up your pension if you become a member of an employer's pension scheme through additional voluntary contributions (AVCs).

Many couples choose to live together nowadays rather than marry. For some it is just a transitionary period before marriage, but increasingly couples are making it a more permanent arrangement and are not even bothering to marry before having children. However, women in this situation should be very careful not to let their hearts rule their heads otherwise they could lose out financially. The advantage of marriage is that it is an institution recognised and upheld by law, so it gives women various rights in respect of property and inheritance. Although many people believe that if they live together long enough they will be treated as common law husband and wife, this is not the case. The term common law marriage has had no legal meaning since 1753. If a dispute over property and finance arises, the law may not be able to take your special relationship into account and women can often end up the losers. A possible way to avoid future problems is to

LIVING TOGETHER-HOW WOMEN CAN LOSE OUT

draw up an agreement right at the start detailing each partner's rights and duties to the other covering such matters as:

Each person's rights in relation to the home

Who pays the mortgage and other household expenses

Who owns the contents of the home

The financial arrangements if one partner stops work to look after children, including pension provision

POSSIBLE PITFALLS

The home

If you move into a property already owned by your partner, you will have very few rights either to continue living or to a gain a financial share in its value if the relationship breaks down - unless you have children. If you have children, a court will consider their needs first and how they can best be provided with a home.

If not, your partner can ask you to leave at any time subject to reasonable notice. He may sell the property at any time without your consent. Only if you can show that you have made a direct and substantial contribution towards the cost of the house,e.g. paid half the mortgage (not just the grocery bills), are you likely to be in a stronger position.

Even better is to have the property transferred into joint names. If you do this or start off by buying a property together, the courts will normally assume the property is owned equally.

Pension rights

Unlike a married woman, if you separate you are unlikely to succeed in claiming a share in your partner's pension benefits. Nor will you have any automatic right to a pension or lump sum if he dies unless he has specifically requested that you should benefit, and then it may still be at the trustees' discretion if it is an employer's scheme. You will not be entitled to a widow's pension from the state either. You may be entitled to other state benefits such as income support but these are normally means tested, whereas widow's benefits are not.

On death

Apart from missing out on a widow's pension, you will also have few automatic rights to the rest of his estate either unless he has named you in his will. Otherwise the rules of intestacy will apply (see Chapter 10). However, if he had been maintaining you wholly or in part prior to his death, you may be able to make a claim under the Inheritance (Provision for Family and Dependants) Act 1975.

If you have children, they will benefit

Your dead partner's estate will be divided equally between his children, whether legitimate or illegitimate.

What happens to your home will depend on the form of joint ownership. There are two possibilities - you can be joint tenants or tenants in common. If you are joint tenants, it means that when one dies the remaining partner automatically acquires full ownership of the property. If you are tenants in common, the dead person's share in the house passes to his or her estate. It is a good idea to opt for this form of ownership, if you have children from a previous relationship whom you want to inherit your share of the property.

DIVORCE - SOME THINGS WOMEN SHOULD BEAR IN MIND

Few husbands and wives come through a divorce financially unscathed. The cost of legal proceedings and the expense of maintaining two households instead of one can leave both partners struggling to make ends meet.

Each divorce is different and the financial arrangements will be determined by a variety of factors, such as whether you have children, your age and employment prospects. Generally speaking, assets acquired after marriage are likely to be split in half. If you have children, what happens to the family home will be considered in the light of what is best for them. The parent caring for the children will normally be allowed to remain in the property until they have finished their education. Then the home may have to be sold and the proceeds shared. However, the question of how mortgage payments will be met will also have to be considered. If you foresee difficulties arising, contact your building society for advice.

A former husband will be expected to provide maintenance for children but wives with jobs or the ability to take jobs are likely to be encouraged by the courts to support themselves. However, you should ensure that enough maintenance is paid to enable you to take out a term assurance policy on your former husband's life to protect the financial welfare of your children while they are growing up.

Pensions:
While you may not qualify for maintenance now, you should think ahead to your retirement. Your husband may have spent decades paying into his employer's pension scheme or his own personal pension plan. His pension could be his most valuable financial asset, while you may have spent many years looking after the children and in

part-time jobs where you did not build up any pension rights. Had you stayed together you would have enjoyed the benefit of your husband's pension. So make sure it is taken into account in the financial arrangements on divorce.

Your husband's National Insurance Contributions will still count towards your state pension for any period in which you were not paying contributions or receiving credits until the year of your divorce.

Death:

Remember divorce cancels any will you or your former husband have made, but you may still have a claim on his estate if he has been supporting you and your children.

Tax:

If you are working after your separation and still have a child living with you, you will be able to claim an additional personal allowance in the year in which you separate. If you separated from your husband after 15 March 1988, any maintenance payments you receive from him are tax free.

It may sound morbid, but married women should start thinking about widowhood as early as possible. In most marriages, husbands predecease their wives and this could occur at any time either as a result of accident or illness. Unless you are prepared this could result in extreme financial hardship for you and your family. With a joint mortgage and children to support, for example, managing on state benefits or just one person's earnings can be extremely difficult.

If you are older and approaching retirement, it is very important to be involved in your husband's

WIDOWHOOD

pension choices. With a personal pension scheme and some types of company schemes, he may be given options regarding a widow's pension.

Life Assurance:

Find out how much life assurance your husband has. You may be entitled to a lump sum from his employer's scheme if he dies before retirement. This will typically be worth three to four times his annual earnings. Check that your mortgage and any other large debts are covered. Get your husband to top up his life cover if necessary. Ask him to put the policy in trust for you so that the money passes to you promptly on his death. (For more details on how to calculate the amount of life cover you require and what types of policies are available, see Chap. 7.)

Pension:

Find out what benefits you can expect from your husband's pension scheme or personal pension plan before and after his retirement. If he dies before retirement a company scheme will normally provide you with a widow's pension based on his contributions up to the time of his death. With a personal pension plan, a lump sum equivalent to his contributions plus investment growth will normally be paid into his estate. Again, ask him to put the plan in trust for you so that the money passes to you promptly on his death. If he dies after retirement, an employer's pension scheme will usually continue to pay you a reduced pension of, say, 50% its previous level. With a personal pension scheme, and with some employers' schemes of the money purchase type, your husband will be able to choose which type of annuity

he buys. So make sure he takes your needs
into account and takes a joint life annuity
which continues after his death preferably on
an increasing basis.

Wills:

Many wives assume they will automatically
inherit all their husbands' assets. But unless
your husband makes a will this may not
necessarily be so under the rules of intestacy
- you may end up having to share his estate
with your mother-in-law (see Chapter 10 for
details). So persuade your husband to make a
will if he has not done so already. This is also
likely to help speed up the legal formalities
after his death.

12   *Financial adviser.*

The main purpose of this book has been to help you assess your own financial goals and explore ways of achieving them. But there are times when you may need professional help. So who can you turn to for advice? Nowadays there are a wide variety of financial advisers around. Some are better equipped to give advice on certain matters, and it often pays to seek two or three different opinions before making your final decision.

In the past, many people have felt uncertain about approaching advisers because they felt they couldn't always be sure about the advisers' level of expertise or honesty, or whether they were getting only one company's view or a recommendation that was influenced by the level of remuneration the adviser was receiving.

Fortunately, because of the Financial Services Act, investors can now feel more confident about the competence and financial stability of the advisers they approach. Only those authorised as 'fit and proper' and with sufficient training are allowed to sell financial products. They must also disclose at the beginning of their meeting with you whether they sell the products of just one company or are independent. They must hand you a Terms of Business which explains their status.

Furthermore, since January 1995, all sellers of policies with an investment element must provide customers with much more information about the product they have recommended, the costs involved and why they think it is suitable for your needs. They must supply you with at least the following information:

A key features document, including the cost of services and the sales person's remuneration

The reasons why the product has been chosen

Key features document
This must explain in plain English, the aims, risks and benefits of the product so that you can gain a clear understanding of how it works. In addition you will get a personal illustration showing how the company's charges and expenses will affect the benefits you receive and how much money you are likely to get back at various times if you surrender your policy.
The sales person will have to tell you the costs of services and remuneration he or she will receive in cash terms both before and after you sign on the dotted line.
For companies which don't pay sales-based commission to their staff, this amount will include among other costs, a proportion of the sales person's basic salary and performance bonuses, the cost of training, equipment, premises and support staff involved.

Reason why
The sales person must write down the reason why a particular product is appropriate to your needs before any sale is made (this applies only to regular premium policies).

One of the advantages of buying financial products through a company representative or independent financial adviser is that you will be able to gain redress if you have received 'bad advice'. If you send off for products that you see advertised or as a result of a direct mail shot, you won't be covered. This is known as 'execution-only' business. If, however, the advertisement or mail shot turns out to be misleading, you will have cause for redress.

This chapter deals with the main sources of advice and then looks at where you can go if you have a complaint about a financial product or service.

INDEPENDENT
FINANCIAL ADVISERS

All these advisers must have been approved by the Personal Investment Authority (PIA). You can check they are authorised by contacting the Securities and Investment Board on 0171 929 3652. Never deal with an IFA who is not fully authorised because you will not be eligible for compensation if something goes wrong.

IFAs can sell you the products of any financial company in the market. They have to keep up to date with what is on offer so they are in a good position to 'shop around' on your behalf. They may not necessarily recommend the cheapest product if they consider that the terms and conditions of another is better for your needs, or they know that another company is more sympathetic in dealing with claims or has a better investment performance record.

Some advisers are authorised to deal in certain products such as life assurance, pensions and unit trusts only, others can give on-going investment advice. They may offer discretionary unit trust services, or their own broker managed investment bonds. Some offer a share dealing service (but then they must be also authorised by the Securities & Futures Authority (SFA)). They may also help with the taxation aspects of your investments, such as recommending when 'bed-and-breakfasting' is necessary to take advantage of your capital gains tax allowance and providing you with the information you need for the taxman at the end of each tax year, in the form of schedules of transactions and dividend payments.

Some major players provide all round financial planning services and can advise you on your life assurance, pensions and investment needs, taking into account taxation aspects as well, such as estate planning.

IFAs receive payment for the time and effort they spend examining your affairs and advising you what to do either via a commission payment from the financial institution whose products they have sold you or on a fee basis. They will either charge a fixed fee or an hourly rate for their advice like accountants or solicitors. You will also be charged if you employ an adviser to undertake discretionary management of your investments. This will usually be an annual percentage charge based on the value of your investments.

Good advisers in this category have much to recommend them. They are independent. They have a good overview of the whole industry, they are normally happy to deal with smaller investors and know that their survival depends on giving a good service. Unless you are given a reliable recommendation, you can get the names of the independent financial advisers in your area by ringing IFA Promotions Ltd. on 0171 831 4027.

In spite of increased regulation, nobody can guarantee that some advisers will not go astray. Although there is a compensation fund in case an adviser is negligent in advising you or goes bust, it should not make you complacent. One way of ensuring temptation does not come an adviser's way is to make all your cheques out to the unit trust group or insurance company concerned. Choosing an advisory service rather than discretionary management also means that you can keep control over your money but you must then make the investment decisions.

COMPANY REPRESENTATIVES

Many insurance companies have built up their own sales force to promote their products and services to the public. The large industrial insurers, such as the Prudential, the Pearl and the Co-operative, have used this method of selling and collecting premiums for many years and their representatives have had a good public image.

During the 1970s when many new unit-linked insurance companies were formed, the number of people selling life assurance and related services increased dramatically. This increasing competition resulted in the use of fairly aggressive sales techniques by some company representatives and there were a number of abuses. Nowadays, however, representatives have to be thoroughly trained, and in many cases they are licensed to sell specific products and are required to obey much tighter rules. Their company has to take full responsibility for their actions, so if anything goes wrong, you will have a resort to the company itself which, if it is keen to protect its reputation, will be anxious to put things right. The new financial services legislation lays down some stiff rules of conduct which all company representatives are obliged to follow and today's representatives operate in a very different world from that of the early 70s.

The advantage that representatives do have is a thorough knowledge of their own company's products. With increasing diversification by financial services groups these are likely to include not only life assurance and pension policies, but also unit trusts, personal equity plans and other products as well. Since representatives are now only allowed to promote the products of their own company, most companies have been anxious to ensure that their representatives have as full a portfolio of products as possible to offer.

Another advantage that a representative has is the technical back-up of his company. The world of financial services has grown increasingly more complex over recent years and the better companies now ensure that their representatives are supported by legal and technical services departments that can provide ready answers to the many technical problems that can arise.

The drawback of dealing with company representatives, however, is that they will only be able to advise you about and sell you the products of their own company, unlike an independent intermediary who should be able to recommend the best company in each product area. So it will be up to you to establish the company's competitiveness, either by asking the representative to show you independent surveys of its results or by checking yourself in magazines such as *Money Management* or

Money Observer.

Nevertheless, no single company provides the best products in every area, and there may also be certain products which a company does not offer. For example, a wholly unit-linked insurance company will not be able to provide with-profits contracts and may not offer annuities. A with-profits company may not offer unit trusts. So, dealing with one company's representative alone could give you a one-sided view, though if the representative's company does not offer a particular product he will be able to direct you towards an independent adviser who might be able to help you.

Company representatives are remunerated in different ways. Some earn commission on each sale they make, others receive a basic salary with commission as a top-up.

TIED AGENTS

Tied agents or appointed representatives also sell just one company's products so they are much the same as company representatives except that they are not employed by the company. They are separate companies or self-employed individuals who have chosen to sell the products of a particular company and receive commission for doing so.

BANKS AND BUILDING SOCIETIES

Most banks and building societies no longer restrict themselves to their traditional roles of providing cash accounts. The larger banks and building societies have set up their own financial services companies offering their own range of insurance and pension products as well as unit trusts and personal equity plans. They are sometimes described as 'bancassurers'. Other banks and building societies have become tied agents and sell the products of one insurance company.

Only a handful have opted to be independent financial advisers, though many of the larger banks and building societies do have IFA divisions. So if you want independent advice you can ask for it.

However, the bancassurers have become increasingly pro-active in selling financial products. Direct mail, letters, phone calls, 'personal bankers' and 'financial consultants' are now used to encourage customers to discuss their financial affairs. Although sales staff receive a basic salary, targets are normally set and performance bonuses given to encourage them to generate as much business as possible. Like other company representatives, they can only sell you what their company offers.

Some of the banks and building societies also offer low cost sharedealing over the telephone or by post. These are mainly execution-only services so no advice is given on which shares you should buy, though some of the banks will provide information and advice on request at no extra charge.

Other traditional services offered by the banks include safe deposit facilities and trustee services.

ACCOUNTANTS

Accountants are usually the best source of advice on tax matters. But don't forget to check their credentials. Currently anyone can set up in business as a 'tax accountant' without having passed a single examination. Some accountants can also give advice on investment matters providing they are authorised by a recognised professional body (such as the Institute of Chartered Accountants) and this type of business is only a small proportion of their overall activities.

Some of the larger firms of accountants have established specialist independent financial advice departments to deal with this side of their business, while others have teamed up with other independent intermediaries to offer a service. Those accountants who do not offer investment advice will be able to provide you with the names of IFAs who can help you.
You will have to pay a fee if you ask an accountant for advice but any commission generated as a result of this advice can be offset against your fees.

SOLICITORS

For advice on legal matters you should turn to a firm of solicitors. They may also be able to provide investment advice if authorised to do so by their professional body. They will charge a fee for their advice but any commission they receive will be deducted. If they do not provide investment advice, they will be able to introduce you to advisers who can.

STOCKBROKERS

The role of stockbrokers has changed considerably in recent years. In the past they tended to cater only for the wealthy. But nowadays with increased competition they are making themselves more accessible to smaller investors, offering PEPs, and unit trust and investment trust management services as well as straightforward sharedealing. A new generation of stockbroker has also sprung up which offers sharedealing services over the telephone and some banks and building societies now offer low cost stockbroking services.

Stockbrokers may offer three types of services:

Execution only

This is the cheapest service because the broker simply carries out your instructions - buying or selling whichever stocks or shares you say. The charge or commission for these deals will depend on the value of the transaction, though all brokers will set a minimum commission of, say £20.

Advisory

This service may be available on various levels. A broker may be prepared to give you once-off advice on which gilt stocks to buy, for example, or he may offer a full blown advisory management service recommending which shares you should buy or sell for your portfolio. Another version of this type of service is where a stockbroker provides general information bulletins about shares with buy, sell or hold recommendations which you can act on if you wish to do so.

Discretionary

With this type of service, you give your stockbroker discretion to buy and sell investments on your behalf, having agreed your requirements beforehand.

To find out which stockbrokers are happy to deal with private investors, contact the Association of Private Client Investment Managers and Shareholders and request a free copy of the national directory of private client stockbrokers.

PROBLEMS AND
COMPLAINTS

If you feel you have been maltreated or misled by a financial institution or anyone else in the financial services industry, there are a number of complaints procedures and ombudsmen you can turn to for help. If an ombudsman deems your complaint to be justified he can award compensation, but you are not normally bound to accept his decision and can still challenge the company in the courts if you wish to do so.

But first you will need to go through the internal complaints procedure of the institution concerned. Remember to keep copies of all your letters and the original documents (only send copies of these documents with your correspondence). If you are not satisfied, contact the chief executive and ask for a reply within a reasonable time period. If still dissatisfied, find out which complaints scheme covers the organisation involved. Write to the relevant body with an explanation of your dispute. Make sure you do this reasonably quickly as some schemes limit the time available to register your complaint typically to six months after you received a final answer from the organisation concerned.

The Banking Ombudsman:
This scheme covers 38 UK banks, including all the high street banks. The ombudsman has the power to make binding awards of up to £100,000 and will deal with all types of banking business normally transacted through bank branches. Cash machines, credit cards, loans, mortgages and overdrafts are covered (but only where a mistake has been made, not in connection with a bank's commercial judgement). He will deal with problems concerning executor and trustee services and some aspects of a bank's insurance services.

The scheme is open to individuals, clubs, sole traders, partnerships and small companies with less than £1m turnover.

The Building Society Ombudsman:
Most complaints about building societies are handled by this ombudsman if they concern mortgages, other loans, savings accounts, banking services, trusteeship and executorship. But it does not normally deal with decisions relating to creditworthiness, or cases that are, or have been, the subject of court proceedings. To be eligible complaints must be brought by an existing customer of a building society who has personally suffered loss or inconvenience by a society's action. All building societies are covered by this scheme and the ombudsman can recommend compensation of up to £100,000. However, societies are not forced to accept his decision, though if they don't they must publish their reasons in the press. So far only one society has refused to comply.

The Corporate Estate Agents Ombudsman:
Unfortunately, this scheme covers only the larger estate agency chains such as Hamptons, not independent estate agents. The ombudsman can make binding awards of up to £100,000 and will consider complaints about members concerning infringement of legal rights, unfair treatment and maladministration resulting in loss or inconvenience. He will not consider complaints about surveys.

The Insurance Ombudsman:
All complaints about general insurance matters - such as motor, household, holiday, personal accident and health insurance policies - are dealt with by the ombudsman. He can make binding awards of up to

£100,000 on the members of the scheme which include most insurance companies and Lloyd's of London. However, he will not deal with matters which are the subject of legal proceedings, a commercial decision, or premium levels.

The Pensions' Ombudsman:
Problems concerning employers' pension schemes can be taken to this ombudsman, but you must approach the Occupational Pensions Advisory Service (OPAS) first to see if the matter can be sorted out. If you are still dissatisfied, you can take the matter up with the ombudsman who deals with disputes and complaints about maladministration by trustees and managers of pension schemes. Eligible complainants include members of pension schemes or their widows, widowers or dependants. The scheme does not cover public service pension schemes, with the exception of the NHS scheme. There is no limit on the amount of compensation the ombudsman can award but his decision is binding on both parties.

The Personal Investment Authority Ombudsman:
This ombudsman has a wide scope, broadly across all products with an investment content, including life assurance, personal pensions, unit trusts, Personal Equity Plans, investment trust saving and investment schemes, recognized offshore funds, broker funds, management of portfolios and more. He can make binding awards of up to £50,000 if a company has broken any of the PIA's rules or code of conduct. He can recommend higher awards if he thinks fit.

Other complaints procedures include the Inland Revenue's independent adjudicator who can

deal with taxpayers' complaints about the way
their tax affairs have been handled, and those of
professional and regulatory bodies, such as the
Securities & Futures Authority which regulates
stockbrokers.

Useful addresses

Association of British Insurers
51 Gresham Street
London EC2V 7HQ
071 600 3333
Supplies a range of useful leaflets on different types of insurance

Association of Investment Trust Companies
Park House (6th Floor)
16 Finsbury Circus
London EC2M 7JJ
071 588 5347
Supplies wide range of data about investment trusts

Association of Private Client Investment Managers and Shareholders
20 Dysart Street
London EC2A 2BX
071 247 7080
Supplies national directory of private client stockbrokers

Association of Unit Trusts and Investment Funds
65 Kingsway
London WC2B 6TD
071 831 0898
Various factsheets and other information available

Independent Schools Information Service
56 Buckingham Gate
London SW1E 6AG
071 630 8793
Leaflets on schools, school fees, grants and assisted places available

Inland Revenue
(For local office, see telephone directory)
Supplies variety of useful free leaflets and booklets, ask for catalogue listing all those available

Proshare
13-14 Basinghall Street
London EC2V 5BQ
071 600 0984
Provides information about investing in shares

Banking Ombudsman   COMPLAINTS
70 Grays Inn Road
London WC1X 8NB
071 404 9944

Building Societies Ombudsman
Grosvenor Gardens House
35-37 Grosvenor Gardens
London SW1X 7AW
071 931 0044

Corporate Estate Agents Ombudsman
Old Library Chambers
21 Chipper Lance

Salisbury
Wilts SP1 1YQ
0722 333306

Insurance Ombudsman Bureau
135 Park Street
London SE1 9EA
071 928 7600

Pensions Ombudsman
11 Belgrave Road
London SW1V 1RB
071 834 9144

Personal Investment Authority Ombudsman
6th Floor
1 London Wall
London EC2Y 5EA
071 600 3838

Revenue Adjudicator's Office
3rd Floor
Haymarket House
28 Haymarket
London SW1Y 4SP

OTHER USEFUL
ADDRESSES

Institute of Chartered Accountants in England & Wales
Chartered Accountants Hall
Moorgate Place
London EC2P 2BJ

Institute of Chartered Accountants in Scotland
27 Queen Street
Edinburgh EH2 1LA

Chartered Association of Certified Accountants
29 Lincoln's Inn Fields
London WC2A 3EE

Occupational Pensions Advisory Service
11 Belgrave Road,
London SW1V 1RB

The Register of Pension Schemes
Occupational Pensions Board
PO Box 1NN
Newcastle-upon-Tyne NE99 1NN

The Royal Institute of Chartered Surveyors
12 Great George Street
London SW1P 3AE

The Securities & Futures Authority
12 Old Broad Street
London EC2

The Securities & Investment Board
2 Bunhill Row
London EC1Y 8RA

The Law Society
Ipsley Court
Barrington Close
Redditch
Worcestershire
B98 0TD

Index

women and 174-6
personal tax allowances
basic personal allowance 83, 84
blind person's allowance 83, 84
higher age related allowance 83, 84, 94
married couples allowance 83, 84, 85-6
single parent allowance 83, 84
Premium Bonds 44, 89
property trusts 56
ProShare 58
publications
Business Moneyfacts 20, 145
Investment Trusts 53
Money Management 49, 52, 55, 79, 189
Money Observer 43, 52, 53, 58, 79
Moneyfacts 20, 42, 43, 70
Which? 20

R

redundancy: reviewing your investments 64
retirement
age allowance 'trap' 94
early retirement and your pension 111-12
reclaiming tax 94
reviewing your investments 64-5
tax efficient strategies 93-4
taxation in 93-4
see also pensions
risk and reward 37-41
balanced portfolio 36, 39-40
high risk investments 39, 56-61
low risk investments 38, 39, 41-8
medium risk investments 39, 48-56
risk reduction 38-9
time-scale 38

S

Save-As-You-Earn share option schemes 45-6
school fees 155-60
approximate costs 156
borrowing to finance 159
educational trusts 158
lump sum investment 157
payments protection schemes 155
planning for 155
regular savings schemes 156-7
school composition fees 158-9
secured loans 25, 32-3
Securities & Futures Authority (SFA) 187, 197
Securities and Investment Board 186
self-employment 142-53
banking 144
business expenses 87, 147
Enterprise Allowance 143-4
entitlement to state benefits 150-1

grant/loan schemes 145
life assurance and health insurance 152-3
making the transition 143
mortgages 143
pensions see personal pension plans
raising finance 144-5
small business insurance policy 153
taxation 87, 146-9
trading losses 147
using an accountant 148, 149
SERPS *see* state earnings related pension schemes
shares
blue chip companies 57
buying 57
minimum investment 57-8
preference shares 74
risks and returns 57
Save-As-You-Earn share option schemes 45-6
share options 58-9
shareholders' perks 57
tax tip 58
taxation of dividends 58
telephone dealing services 57
sickness benefit 9, 150
solicitors 167, 192
standing orders 21
state benefits
low income/unemployment benefits 151
maternity allowance 150
retirement pension 151
sickness/incapacity benefit 9, 150
widows' benefits 151
state earnings related pension schemes (SERPS)
opting back into 174
opting out of 107-8, 173-4
pension payable 102
women and 173-4
state retirement pension
basic state pension 100-1, 172-3
early retirement 111-12
retirement age 100
for the self-employed 151
SERPS *see* state earnings related pension schemes
for women 171-4
women's career breaks 176
stockbrokers 192-3
advisory service 193
discretionary service 193
execution only service 193
store cards 29
student loans 159

T

taxation 82-96